BUS REVIEW

14 Review of 1998
Published 1999

GW00401834

from the PS-type to the ALX300. The last PS went to Stagecoach and is seen here with the first production ALX300. Both are on Volvo chassis. *Alexander*

Front cover: The first new buses for Capital Citybus under FirstGroup ownership were 17 Volvo Olympians which had been ordered while the company was still independent. They had Northern Counties bodies. *SJB*

Back cover, upper: The most surprising additions to a Stagecoach fleet in Britain were three-axle Dennis Dragons which were transferred to Stagecoach Manchester from Nairobi. They were painted in Magic Bus livery. *SJB*

Back cover, lower: The first new double-deckers to carry Arriva corporate colours were 13 DAFs for Arriva London & Country, used to replace older double-deckers on the London Transport service between Kingston and Putney. They had dual-door 67-seat Northern Counties Palatine II bodies. *Peter Rowlands*

Contents

Van Hool's new T9 Alizee appeared in many fleets during 1998. One of the biggest orders came from Shearings, which took 15 on Volvo B10M chassis. *David Barrow*

First published 1999
ISBN 0 946265 30 5
© Bus Enthusiast Publishing Company, 1999
Typeset in Times and Helvetica
Electronic page makeup by Jeremy Scott
Printed by Pillans & Wilson, Edinburgh

Published by
Bus Enthusiast Publishing Company
5 Hallcroft Close, Ratho, Newbridge
Midlothian EH28 8SD
Bus Enthusiast is an imprint of
Arthur Southern Ltd.

All rights reserved.
Except for normal review purposes, no part of
this book may be reproduced in any form or
by any means, electronic or mechanical,
including photocopying, recording or by any
information storage and retrieval system
without the written permission of the
publishers who have no arrangement with any
agency to permit any such copying.

Introduction

It was another exciting year in the bus and coach industry in 1998, as the pages which follow will show. There may have been fewer take-overs than in the early part of the 1990s, but some of those which happened in 1998 were particularly interesting. FirstGroup bought Mainline, marking significant expansion for the group in Yorkshire. Metroline bought MTL London and then Scottish Citylink; FirstGroup bought Capital Citybus – all further reducing the number of operators competing for tenders in the capital.

Having said that a new name did appear in London – Travel London – while others expanded, notably Thorpe and Capital Logistics.

The crash of Q Drive in the autumn had repercussions on London's bus services, while the sale of its fleet of modern coaches meant that there were some good buys to be had in time for the 1999 coaching season, even if that proves to be bad news for those selling new coaches. Other less widely publicised operators in trouble included Border Buses of Burnley, in administrative receivership, and Ralphs of Langley, which closed.

Other companies to experience changes of ownership included Kinchbus (to Wellglade), Village Tours of Liverpool (to MTL North), Pathfinder of Newark (to Nottingham City Transport) and Oban & District (to West Coast Motors).

New coach designs appeared on Britain's roads in 1998 including the latest Van Hool Alizee, the Caetano Enigma, the Berkhof Radial, the first Smit Orion and Plaxton's diminutive Cheetah. And more new models

were announced for 1999, including the re-entry of Ayats to the British market. A new coach chassis maker appeared from Northern Ireland, Cannon, and got off to a slow start.

Among the manufacturers, Plaxton and Dennis were about to be wed when Mayflower, owners of Walter Alexander, decided to get involved. The result? The wedding was called off, and Dennis ended up with Alexander as its new partner. And just as everyone was expecting UVG at Waterlooville to quietly disappear, Caetano mounted a rescue and kept the operation going as SC Coachbuilders.

Trams were in the news, with Stagecoach taking over Sheffield Supertram and work continuing apace on Croydon Tramlink, due to open towards the end of 1999. The Midland Metro should have opened in 1998 but didn't. There's growing interest in guided busways too, particularly in Edinburgh, Northampton and Liverpool.

The double-decker of the future – fully accessible to wheelchair users – made its debut at the start of the year, with the numbers entering service accelerating as the year progressed. The last two-step double-deckers for UK service were under construction as the year ended.

Arriva's corporate colours spread slowly, while FirstGroup stuck to its strange twin-livery policy with corporate colours being applied only to new corporate buses. However with almost 600 corporate-liveried buses taking to the streets in 1998 the new look was certainly having some impact.

Interesting overseas happenings included FirstGroup winning a major franchise in Hong Kong and setting up New World First Bus, and Stagecoach shipping three-axle Dennis Dragons from Kenya to Manchester and refurbishing them for UK service.

To keep up with events in Britain's fast-changing bus and coach businesses the pages of the monthly magazine *Buses* provide first-class coverage, while for those wanting real detail membership of the PSV Circle with a subscription to its News Sheets is recommended. For a snap-shot of current fleets, British Bus Publishing's Bus Handbooks provide fleet lists for all major and many smaller operators throughout the British Isles.

Stewart J Brown
Reedley Hallows, 1999

Coach of the Year at the 1998 Brighton rally was this EOS owned by Hallmark Coaches. *SJB*

Arriva arrives

ARRIVA'S NEW corporate image was unveiled towards the end of 1997 and it spread fairly rapidly during 1998. But more than liveries changed, as Arriva renamed all of its bus operating subsidiaries at the start of April, as shown in the list on page 6. Generally, clearly identifiable geographic names were selected, the only real exception being Arriva Fox County. The legal lettering on the sides of buses was changed in the spring to reflect the companies' new names.

Expansion by Arriva was focused on mainland Europe, with the acquisition of a majority shareholding in Vancom Nederland in January being followed in November by two further Dutch acquisitions, Veonn and Hanze, from the state-owned VSN Group. In Holland the group operates as Arriva Nederland.

There was modest expansion in Britain, although some of it proved contentious. In March Arriva the Shires took over the operations of Lutonian Bus which ran 20

minibuses. Before giving up, Lutonian had complained to the Office of Fair Trading about unfair competition from Arriva the Shires. When the take-over was completed Arriva the Shires closed down its low-cost Challenger operation which had been competing with Lutonian. The take-over was referred to the Monopolies and Mergers Commission in the summer – and in November it instructed Arriva the Shires to sell Lutonian, although this had not happened by the end of the year.

Arriva Fox County replaced 20 per cent of its double-deck fleet in 1998 with the delivery of 38 new Volvo Olympians, one of the biggest orders for new double-deck buses during the year. They had lowheight Northern Counties Palatine I bodies. *SJB*

Seen soon after being acquired by Crosville Wales is an ex-Halton Leyland Lynx in the Devaway fleet. *SJB*

Williamsons of Knockin Heath gave up bus operation in August and among the buses taken over by Arriva Midlands North were two Optare Excels. *SJB*

There were two acquisitions of note in Wales. In March Crosville Wales acquired Devaway which operated 21 vehicles in the Chester area; most were Leyland Nationals and Lynxes. And in August the old-established Purple Motors of Bethesda, running 12 vehicles, was acquired by Arriva Cymru, as the company had by then become.

In April Arriva took over two separate parts of Timeline's business in Shropshire and in the Greater Manchester and Cheshire areas. The Shropshire fleet had 19 buses; Arriva acquired 20 Timeline buses in Greater Manchester. And in August Arriva Midlands North added to its portfolio the seven-strong bus operation of Williamsons Motorways of Knockin Heath. These included two Optare Excels. Williamsons retained its coach operations.

While Arriva picked up a few small bus operations around the country, it divested itself of some of its coaching interests. First to go, in May, was the Star Line coach operation which was sold to Selwyns Travel of Runcorn, with eight vehicles. In September Arriva London & Country sold the former Blue Saloon coach business in Guildford to Countryliner, a new company picking up the existing trading name of London & Country's Guildford-based coach fleet. At the same time Grey-Green – now Arriva London North East – gave up its six-vehicle Essex

Arriva – a reprise

ARRIVA'S ROOTS lie in the Drawlane organisation which first made the news in 1987 when it started bidding for National Bus Company subsidiaries in the privatisation progamme. Drawlane metamorphosed into British Bus in December 1992, and that organisation was taken over by the Cowie motor trade group, based in Sunderland, in the summer of 1996. Cowie already operated buses in London through the ownership of Grey-Green, Leaside and South London Transport, and shortly before buying British Bus had added County Bus & Coach to its portfolio.

All changed at the end of 1997, when the Cowie Group was renamed Arriva and the Arriva identity was applied across the entire interests of the former Cowie organisation – embracing car sales, vehicle rental, bus and coach sales (at Hughes DAF – now Arriva Bus & Coach) and the 7,000-vehicle bus operations.

The main UK bus acquisitions by Drawlane/British Bus/Cowie are shown alongside.

Arriva Acquisitions

1987 Shamrock & Rambler
1988 Midland Red (North)
       London Country South West
       North Western Road Car Co

1989 Crosville
       Bee Line Buzz
       Frontrunner North West
       Midland Fox
       Speedlink Airport Services

1990 Tellings-Golden Miller
       Alder Valley (part)

1991 National Express Group
       (25%, later sold)

1992 Crosville Wales

1993 Colchester Boro' Transport
       Southend Transport
       Liverline

1994 Stevensons
       Proudmutual
            Northumbria
            Kentish Bus
       Luton & District
       Derby City Transport
       Clydeside 2000

1995 *Londonlinks Buses formed*
       Warrington Goldlines
       launched
       Caldaire Holdings
            Selby & District
            South Yorkshire
                 Transport
            West Riding
            Yorkshire Woollen
       Maidstone & District
       Frontline
       Arrowline
            Star Line

1996 North East Bus
            United Auto
            Tees & District
            TMS

1997 London Coaches (part)
       McGill's Bus Service

1998 Timeline (part)

Arriva Cymru was one of eight Arriva companies which between them bought almost 100 Plaxton-bodied Mercedes-Benz in 1998. Arriva Cymru had 25, one of which loads in Chester. *SJB*

commuter coach operations which were taken over by Essex Express, run jointly by three independents – Chambers of Bures, Fargo Coachlines of Rayne and Windmill Coaches of Colchester.

New vehicles for Arriva during 1998 included 60 Northern Counties-bodied Volvo Olympians for Arriva Cymru (seven), Arriva The Shires (15) and Arriva Fox County (38). These were lowheight Palatine Is. Full-height Palatine IIs, on DAF DB250 chassis, were delivered to Arriva London & Country for a London tendered service. All were in corporate colours. Red double-deckers for London operation were the first of an order for 63 two-door low-floor Alexander-bodied DAFs.

Dennis Dart SLFs were delivered to a number of Arriva companies. There were over 100 with Plaxton Pointer bodies, including 43 for Arriva North East. In addition 25 Alexander-bodied Darts were delivered to Arriva Scotland West and Arriva London North East. Full-size single-deckers were mainly low-floor DAFs, of which there were almost 100 delivered in 1998. Plaxton Prestige bodies were specified by Arriva London North and Arriva North East, and Alexander ALX300 bodies by Arriva Yorkshire. The group's last old-style two-step entrance single-deckers were 15 Scania L113s with Plaxton Paladin bodies for Midland Red North and Stevensons.

Around 125 Mercedes minibuses with Plaxton and Alexander bodies were also delivered to a Arriva companies. Optare MetroRiders were bought in smaller numbers by United Auto, Northumbria and Kentish Bus.

No new orders for 1999-2000 were announced by the end of 1998.

ARRIVA ARRIVES: THE NEW NAMES

Arrowline	Arriva Cheshire
Bee Line Buzz Co	Arriva Manchester
Clydeside Buses	Arriva Scotland West
Colchester Borough Transport	Arriva Colchester
County Bus & Coach Co	Arriva East Herts & Essex
Crosville Wales	Arriva Cymru
Derby City Transport	Arriva Derby
Grey-Green	Arriva London North East
Guildford & West Surrey	Arriva Croydon & North Surrey
Invictaway	Arriva Southern Counties
Kentish Bus & Coach Co	Arriva Kent Thameside
LDT	Arriva the Shires
Leaside Bus Co	Arriva London North
Liverline Travel Services	Arriva Merseyside
London & Country	Arriva Crawley & East Surrey
Londonlinks	Arriva Croydon & North Surrey
Lucketts Garage (Watford)	Arriva Watford
Maidstone & District	Arriva Kent & Sussex
Midland Fox	Arriva Fox County
Midland Red North	Arriva Midlands North
North East Bus	Arriva North East
North Western Road Car	Arriva North West
Northumbria Motor Services	Arriva Northumbria
Selby & District Bus Company	Arriva Yorkshire North
South Lancs Transport	Arriva Lancashire
South London Transport	Arriva London South
South Yorkshire Road Transport	Arriva Yorkshire South
Southend Borough Transport	Arriva Southend
Tees & District Transport	Arriva Tees & District
Teesside Motor Services	Arriva Teesside
Unibus, Denmark	Arriva Danmark
United Automobile Services	Arriva Durham County
Vancom Nederland	Arriva Nederland
West Riding Automobile	Arriva Yorkshire
Yorkshire Woollen District	Arriva Yorkshire West

Unchanged names
Eden Bus Services
Leaside Travel
London Coaches (to 6/98)
The Original London Sightseeing Tour (from 6/98)
Lutonian Buses
McGills
New Enterprise Coaches
Stevensons of Uttoxeter

Alexander launches the ALX100 - again

IN THE SUMMER of 1997 Alexander replaced its established AM Sprint minibus body with the new ALX100. The change coincided with the arrival of the new Mercedes-Benz Vario chassis.

The ALX100 was an improvement on the Sprint, with square-cornered gasket glazing and a neat rear end with recessed circular lights, a styling cue picked up from the ALX200. But the body profile with its straight sides suggested that under the skin the ALX100 was little more than a face-lifted Sprint and the only significant buyer for the new model was the Cowie group.

And so, 12 months later, in the summer of 1998, a second ALX100 appeared, still on the Mercedes Vario chassis. Underneath the skin

the structure was little altered, but moulded skirt panels took away the slab-sided look of the original model, and the glazing was altered with distinctive finishing strips top and bottom. The result? A new-look ALX100 with a style to match the best.

By 1998 Cowie had become Arriva, and it was Arriva which got the first 30 of the new ALX100s,

but Stagecoach took some too – 40 for operation in Devon, Oxford, Cumberland and Cleveland.

The vast majority of AM Sprints were bought by big operators, and initial indications are that the ALX100 is being built in response to fleet orders – leaving Plaxton's Beaver 2 to continue as the most popular small bus choice among smaller businesses.

Spot the difference. The old (bottom) and new (top) faces of the ALX100. The restyled model has neater glazing, deeper cove panels and some shape to the skirt. The two vehicles also illustrate the change which has taken place since Cowie in 1997 metamorphosed into Arriva in 1998. *SJB*

Arrow's last flight

THE DENNIS ARROW, launched as the Lance double-decker in 1995, came to the end of its short flight in 1998. High-floor double-deck chassis are on their way out and the Arrow is one of the casualties of the switch to low-floor.

The Lance name came from the single-deck chassis, from which the double-decker was developed. However within six months the new Dennis double-decker was rechristened the Arrow – although not till after the first had actually entered service with Lance badges.

The first Lance double-decker, with Northern Counties Palatine II body for Nottingham City Transport, was exhibited at Coach & Bus 95. Nottingham bought four.

The 10.5m-long Arrow was, in theory at least, a genuine 100-passenger double-decker – a figure achievable with 84 seats and 16 standees in East Lancs-bodied examples.

The biggest buyer of Arrows was Capital Citybus, attracted by the fuel economy of the Cummins C-series engine. The company reckoned that the Arrow was up to 2mpg more economical than other un-named types in its fleet – which by implication meant the Volvo Olympian. Capital Citybus operates 56 Arrows with Northern Counties Palatine II and East Lancs Pyoneer bodywork. Other London area operators which bought Arrows were London Traveller, which took one with East Lancs Pyoneer body in 1998, and London & Country which was an early Arrow buyer with 10 in 1996 which had old-style East Lancs bodywork.

The only other bus operator to buy Arrows was Aintree Coachline with two, one bodied by Northern Counties, the other by East Lancs. However a further two were built for use as playbuses, with bodywork by East Lancs.

In all, Dennis built 75 Arrows. The model maintained a Dennis presence in the UK double-deck market between the demise of the Dominator and the appearance of the Trident. And the Trident is clearly the model to watch. Before the first had entered service Dennis had over 300 orders. History will mark the Arrow as an interim model, the one which enthusiasts will be travelling the country to seek out in 15 years time when its rarity value is truly appreciated.

• 1998 also saw the end of Dennis Dragon production, with the last chassis being shipped to Hong Kong for Kowloon Motor Bus. It will enter service in 1999. The Dragon was a three-axle chassis based on the UK market Dominator.

ARROW BUYERS	
Aintree Coachline	2
Capital Citybus	56
London & Country	10
London Traveller	1
Nottingham	4
Playbuses	2
TOTAL	75

Capital Citybus is the biggest user of Dennis Arrows. In 1998 it took 28 with East Lancs bodies for use on two newly-won LT contracts. *SJB*

New in Scotland

The first lowheight versions of the East Lancs Pyoneer body were supplied to Strathtay Scottish on Volvo Olympian chassis. *Billy Nicol*

Berkhof's new Radial body found a few buyers in 1998. Among the first was this one on a Dennis Javelin chassis for Lothian Region Transport. It was LRT's first Berkhof body; in recent years the company has bought Caetano-bodied Javelins. *Billy Nicol*

While Marshall's integral Minibus looks set to disappear, the company more than compensated by bodying an increasing number of Darts. Coakley of Motherwell took Darts with both Marshall and Plaxton bodies. A Marshall-bodied bus loads in central Glasgow. *Billy Nicol*

How low can you go?

THE FIRST new-generation low-floor double-deckers to enter revenue-earning service in the UK did so in February. A-Bus of Bristol claimed to be the very first, beating Travel West Midlands by a matter of hours. The first in Scotland was for Travel Dundee, also in February. All three operators, with one bus each, were running Optare Spectras, based on DAF DB250LF chassis.

Indeed, the only low-floor double-deckers to enter service in 1998 were DAFs, with a few more Spectras, and then the first Alexander ALX400s, these being for Arriva London North.

Plaxton's President, star of Coach & Bus 97, did some demonstration work, being shown in Edinburgh, Liverpool, London and Cardiff – but it didn't actually carry passengers and the reckoning is that it never will. The Volvo chassis on which it was based was being extensively re-designed for double-deck operation, and the 1997 show President is unlikely to be seen in public again.

Dennis, whose three-axle export Trident low-floor chassis went into production in 1997, revealed a UK-specification two-axle model in January. The UK Trident is available in two lengths, 9.9 and 10.4m and uses a transverse Cummins C-series engine rated at 220 or 245bhp with a choice of Voith or ZF automatic gearboxes. It also has a step-free gangway for the full length of the lower deck, thanks to the use of a ZF drop-centre rear axle. This allows Tridents to be built with bodywork having an overall height as low as 4.2m.

While the drive-train is quite different from that of the three-axle Trident with its big Cummins M11 engine, there is a high degree of commonality in the area ahead of the rear axle

In May Volvo announced that a new low-floor chassis was coming with what it described as an Olympian-style drivetrain and B10BLE front suspension. Lothian Region Transport ordered six, while Travel West Midlands ordered two. By this time DAF was claiming 150 orders and Dennis almost 300, not counting its Hong Kong business.

The new Volvo chassis was officially launched in August as the B7L. It has a transverse 6.7-litre Volvo D7C engine with a choice of three power ratings, 215, 250 or 290bhp. This is the engine which had been mounted longitudinally in the prototype Plaxton President, a layout which had attracted criticism because of the long rear overhang which it created. The B7L comes with a choice of ZF or Voith automatic gearboxes and the chassis is also suitable for single-deck and articulated buses. Two major orders were announced in 1998 for Go-Ahead subsidiaries London Central and London General, taking 91 between them, all with Alexander ALX400 bodies.

The first B7L chassis were delivered to Northern Counties at the end of 1998. When it made its May announcement Volvo said

that its new double-deck chassis would be built at Irvine. Then in June it announced that Irvine's bus plant would be closing – albeit not for two years.

So British operators can expect their first B7Ls to be Scottish-built, but from some time in 2000 they will find their B7Ls coming from either Sweden or Poland.

While DAF, Dennis and Volvo have all launched low-floor double-deckers, the fourth manufacturer active in the double-deck business, Scania, has as yet expressed no interest in the low-floor 'decker market.

Four bodybuilders are working on low-floor double-deckers: Alexander, East Lancs, Optare and Plaxton.

Alexander is well ahead, thanks in part to its orders from Hong Kong for ALX500s on Dennis Trident chassis. The ALX500 is for three-axle chassis, while two-axle UK-specification buses get the similar ALX400 body. The first ALX400, on a DAF for Arriva's London operations, was unveiled in May, with production examples following from November. Towards the end of the year ALX400s on Dennis Trident chassis for Stagecoach were nearing completion.

Destined never to enter service, Plaxton's pre-production President on a Volvo chassis was shown to a few operators during 1998. It is seen here being evaluated by London Transport at Aldgate in the summer. *Plaxton*

The first low-floor double-deckers to enter service in the north west were two DAFs with Optare Spectra bodies, running for Bullock of Cheadle. Note the Easy Access branding. *SJB*

Optare got off to a flying start, but reported few orders as the year progressed. In sharp contrast Plaxton, side-tracked by the stalled Volvo prototype, was winning sizeable orders but didn't actually deliver any vehicles during 1998 although it built a pre-production President on a DAF DB250 chassis. This used conventional gasket glazing (the 1997 show vehicle had bonded glazing) and this weakened the dramatic appearance of the original body. Both glazing methods will be available on production Presidents which, although being built by Northern Counties, are being badged as Plaxton products. This points to the Northern Counties name disappearing in 1999 as Palatine production comes to an end.

East Lancs, which has been using the Alusuisse method of aluminium extrusions to build single-deck bodies, adopted Alusuisse for its new low-floor double-decker, coded ADD99: Aluminium Double Decker 1999. This was styled by John Worker Design and announced at the end of the year as the Lolyne, a name which not only continues the company's theme of names with a contrived "y" in them, but stirs memories of a Dennis chassis of years gone by.

The first Lolyne, appropriately enough on a Dennis chassis, was completed in December but will not enter service until 1999. It is one of 12 for Nottingham City Transport.

The move to low-floor spells the end for a number of established double-deck models. The last Volvo Citybus entered service in 1997; the last Dennis Arrow in 1998. Expect the last Scania N113 and Volvo Olympian to follow in 1999.

LOW-FLOOR ORDERS: 1998-99

A-Bus, Bristol	2	DAF DB250LF	Optare Spectra
Arriva group	130	DAF DB250LF	Alexander ALX400
Brighton & Hove	20	Dennis Trident	East Lancs Lolyne
Bullock, Cheadle	2	DAF DB250LF	Optare Spectra
Capital Logistics	10	DAF DB250LF	Plaxton President
	6	DAF DB250LF	Optare Spectra
First CentreWest	31	Dennis Trident	Plaxton President
London Central	46	Volvo B7L	Alexander ALX400
London General	45	Volvo B7L	Alexander ALX400
Lothian Region Transport	1	Volvo B7L	Plaxton President
	5	Volvo B7L	TBA
	5	Dennis Trident	Plaxton President
	5	Dennis Trident	Alexander ALX400
Metroline	16	Dennis Trident	Alexander ALX400
	75	Dennis Trident	Plaxton President
Nottingham City Transport	12	Dennis Trident	East Lancs Lolyne
Oxford Bus Company	20	Dennis Trident	Alexander ALX400
Stagecoach	100	Dennis Trident	Alexander ALX400
Travel Dundee	1	DAF DB250LF	Optare Spectra
Travel West Midlands	21	DAF DB250LF	Optare Spectra
	2	Volvo B7L	Plaxton President
Wilts & Dorset	6	DAF B250LF	Optare Spectra
Yellow Buses, Bournemouth	9	Dennis Trident	East Lancs Lolyne

TOTALS	Chassis	Bodies
	DAF – 178	Alexander – 362
	Dennis – 293	East Lancs – 41
	Volvo – 99	Plaxton – 126
	Optare – 38	

Anyone for Dennis?

IT ALL SEEMED straightforward enough – at the start. Britain's biggest bodybuilder, Henlys-owned Plaxton, was merging with Britain's biggest chassis maker, Dennis. The deal was announced at the end of July and the two parties then expected to get on with combining their businesses to create a bus manufacturing group with a £640million turnover.

It looked like a good combination. The ubiquitous Dennis Dart SLF with Plaxton Pointer body is Britain's best-selling bus, and Plaxton is the main bodybuilder on the Dennis Javelin coach chassis – although it builds many more coach bodies on Volvo's market-leading B10M.

Both companies export to the Far East where Dennis has a particularly strong presence, and during 1998 they were working on a deal to supply buses to Canada, including that country's first ever new double-deckers. Both companies said that they saw potential for growth in North America.

The announcement was welcomed by investors, and both companies' share prices shot up by around 10 per cent.

Then in sailed Mayflower.

Mayflower is a multi-faceted automotive group which owns Walter Alexander, acquired in 1995. And Mayflower decided it would like control of Dennis and in mid-August made a bid which valued the company much higher than the Henlys merger proposal – around £254.7million against Henlys' £184million. There were bids and counter bids and a bitter war of words between Henlys and Mayflower. The Dennis Group – which also builds fire engines, refuse collection vehicles and bus body kits through Duple Metsec – continued to support the original plans which, it could be argued, made good long-term sense.

In September Mayflower announced a "strategic alliance" with Daimler-Benz which was strong on impact if short on substance. It talked of joint ventures but gave no hint of what or when.

Volvo got peripherally involved, taking a 10 per cent stake in Henlys and lending its weight to the Henlys-Dennis merger. But in the end Dennis shareholders decided that Mayflower was making an offer too good to refuse – and in October Mayflower took control. Its final bid valued Dennis at £268.9million.

What does it all mean?

In the short term, expect little to change. The Dart SLF/Pointer combination is a winner and neither manufacturer is going to want to jeopardise that. And while Mayflower will no doubt want to see closer links between Alexander and Dennis, it is clearly well aware that traditionally the bulk of Alexander's output has been on Volvo chassis.

However where in the recent past we've seen Dennis and Plaxton working hand-in-glove to build the Super Pointer Dart, using their combined skills to optimise the layout of the complete vehicle, it would seem safe to forecast that any future new Dennis products are more likely to be developed with Alexander as the lead bodybuilder.

And it's hard to see Mayflower standing by to let Dennis/Plaxton attack new markets like Canada, when they have bodybuilding factories in Falkirk and Belfast to keep busy.

Other unsettled business for Mayflower includes the future for Duple Metsec and Alexander (Belfast). In the run-up to taking over the Dennis Group, Mayflower said that it would close Duple Metsec as it already had a kit-producing facility at Alexander, which sends body kits to the Far East for local assembly. However it later seemed to back away from the closure of Duple Metsec – whose fate also has some repercussions for Plaxton, which has been assembling small numbers of Duple Metsec bodies for Hong Kong at its Northern Counties factory in Wigan. There seems little likelihood of that happening in the future.

And Alexander (Belfast) was dealt a major blow in the autumn when Ulsterbus – the factory's main customer – announced that its 1999 body order was going to Wright of Ballymena. That leaves Belfast in 1999 building the last Royales for FirstGroup, and a substantial batch of R-types for Dublin Bus.

It also raises the question of where next for Henlys. Will they seek to form an alliance with another chassis maker? The company already works with Volvo in North America where the two organisations are joint owners of Prevost and Nova Bus.

The wider automotive industry is undergoing change – Daimler-Benz merging with Chrysler, Renault and Iveco combining their bus and coach interests – so Henlys' next move will be watched with interest.

Thamesdown Transport has standardised on the Dennis/Plaxton combination since 1993. Its 1998 delivery comprised 14 of the new 11.3m-long Super Pointer Dart model – a variant announced in 1997. They brought to 54 the number of Darts in Thamesdown's operation. *SJB*

Compass points new direction for Waterlooville

WHEN 1998 DAWNED, the prospects for UVG's Waterlooville coach-building plant looked bleak. The business had been in administrative receivership since December 1997, partly a result of the downturn in demand for buses by the Ministry of Defence, which had been a steady customer for the company's Vanguard body over the years.

Add to that the loss in February of the factory's only substantial contract – the completion of 100 Mercedes O405s for Travel West Midlands – and you couldn't be blamed for writing Waterlooville off. UVG had completed just 10 of the Mercedes; the balance were finished by Mercedes at its engineering operation at Wentworth Park, near Barnsley.

As Wadham Stringer, the company had started to make a slight impression on the bus market at the start of the 1980s. Alongside local authority school and welfare buses, its new Vanguard (launched in 1979) was winning a few orders – for example Scanias for Newport, Tigers for A1 Service, and Ward Dalesmans for Darlington to pick the best-known. It even supplied the National Bus Company, building short Vanguards on Bedford YMQ-S chassis for Eastern National – an order which, it's fair to say, none of the mainstream bodybuilders would probably have wanted.

Wadham Stringer built small numbers of minibuses in the late 1980s and early 1990s, and in 1990 introduced the Portsdown body on the Dennis Dart. It was not a success. Even less successful was the 1993-94 Winchester, a short coach offered on the Dart and on an MAN midi chassis.

In 1993 the company was bought by the Universal Vehicle Group, which was based in West Yorkshire, and renamed WS Coachbuilders. It would be renamed again, becoming UVG, in 1995.

The Vanguard sold steadily to the MoD and a full coach version, on Dennis Javelin chassis, was developed in 1995 as the UniStar, but found few buyers, the best-known being Mayne of Manchester and Go-Whittle of Kidderminster. The UniStar still had something of a utilitarian look about it, and this was addressed in the spring of 1997 with the launch of the S320 which used the Vanguard/UniStar frame with new exterior styling to produce a coach which at a quick glance looked not unlike Plaxton's Premiere. A low price was one of its main selling points – but not low enough to make any significant impact on the market.

Undaunted by poor sales of the Portsdown, Wadham Stringer developed a totally-new body for the low-floor Dart SLF, the UrbanStar. This appeared in 1995 and was a stylish bus (from the studio of John Worker Design), but it was selling in a market where buyers already had plenty of choice and while UrbanStars were more plentiful than Portsdowns, they were hardly commonplace. Southern Vectis bought six on short Dart chassis for a service with a length restriction while Kelvin Central Buses – no doubt to the relief of UVG – snapped up 15 stock vehicles when it was starting to engage in a bus war with Stagecoach in 1997.

But despite the new-look S320 and the competent UrbanStar, the 'For Sale' signs went up at Waterlooville in December 1997 and, to the surprise of many, a buyer came along in April 1998: Caetano.

Renamed SC Coachbuilders, Caetano set about addressing production and quality issues and re-branded the products. In September the S320 became the Cutlass; and the UrbanStar was renamed the Compass. When it took over at Waterlooville, SC Coachbuilders announced that it would build 100 coaches and 200 buses in its first 12 months of production, a figure which sounds a shade optimistic.

UVG continues to build minibuses – the CityStar – at its Bedwas factory in South Wales. The revived UVG operation, SC Coachbuilders, shouldn't be confused with the similar-sounding SC Coachcraft of Mexborough which builds the low-volume Vision coach body on front-engined Mercedes O.817L truck chassis. SC Coachcraft was set up in August 1997.

The UVG S320, seen here, was improved by SC Coachbuilders and relaunched as the Cutlass. David Corbell of London took four UVG-bodied Dennis Javelins in 1998, all in different, but related, liveries.
Peter Rowlands

Out of Africa

ALTHOUGH THE GROUP is never far from the headlines, 1998 was in fact a quiet year for Stagecoach with no significant changes in its UK bus operations.

Its first move, in January, was to take over operation of the Sheffield Supertram, whose uninspiring grey livery was soon being replaced by corporate white-and-stripes. The group's only other UK moves in the bus and rail industries involved taking a 49 per cent stake in Virgin Rail in October, and re-entering the Edinburgh to Glasgow coach market with the takeover of Scottish Highway Express from Owen of Salsburgh. This had been running since May when Owen, a former contractor to Scottish Citylink, decided instead to compete. Stagecoach and Citylink soon came to an agreement which saw a co-ordinated service running between Scotland's two biggest cities.

In July Redby of Sunderland repainted a small number of buses in Stagecoach livery for use on services which it started operating on behalf of Busways.

However while things were quiet on the UK bus front, Stagecoach was making changes overseas. First, it took over Yellow Bus of Auckland, which runs 532 buses. Then it pulled out of Africa. In September the group sold its Kenyan operations. It had been running there since 1991 and had also operated in Malawi between 1989 and 1997. And at the end of the year it was negotiating to buy Hong Kong City Bus, an interesting reversal of the situation a decade ago when Hong Kong City Bus was buying the Ensign Bus operations in London – a connection severed in 1995 but still visible in the HKCB-style yellow livery used by much of the Capital Citybus fleet on the outskirts of London.

Stagecoach's interest in HKCB came after it lost the race to take over the franchises which China Motor Bus was losing.

Stagecoach's withdrawal from Africa had the interesting side-effect of seeing redundant double-deckers being transferred from Nairobi to Manchester – a greater contrast than which is hard to imagine. The buses were three-axle Dennis Tridents with Duple Metsec bodies. For operation in Manchester, more noted for its rain than its sun, the Tridents required some modification.

Two things are essential for any Manchester bus: windscreen wipers and saloon heaters. The Kenyan Dragons had the former but not the latter, so heating had to be installed before they entered service. They retained their deep sliding windows, but with catches to prevent them being fully opened. New moquette seats – 88 of them – have been fitted, and new interior lighting. The other major change involved fitting Cummins L10 engines in place of the original Gardner 6LXCT units. A fleet of 20 Dragons was shipped back to Britain and started to enter service from late autumn in Magic Bus blue.

Elsewhere there were changes taking place as new buses reduced the fleet average age reduced from 7.7 to 7.0 years. Among the new buses were the last Alexander PS types, as deliveries commenced of the low-floor ALX300. Just under 40 PS-types on Volvo B10M chassis were delivered in the early months of the year, most going to

The last Northern Counties Paladin bodies were built by Plaxton at Scarborough in the early part of 1998. Fifty were supplied to four Stagecoach companies including Thames Transit. The chassis was Volvo's mid-engined B10M. *SJB*

Scottish companies. At the start of the year there were 22 ALX300s on Volvo B10BLE chassis for Stagecoach Busways, then from November delivery started of the first of an order for 150 ALX300s on MAN 18.220LE chassis. The first 29 MANs went to Stagecoach Oxford, and were followed by similar buses for Greater Manchester Buses South. A number of companies also received Alexander-bodied Dennis Dart SLFs. Around 150 were delivered with one-third going to London and other sizeable batches being delivered to Thames Transit and Red & White.

Plaxton delivered its last Paladin bodies on Volvo B10M chassis – 50 were shared between Cleveland Transit, GM Buses South, Stagecoach South and Thames Transit.

New double-deckers were 200-plus long-wheelbase Volvo Olympians with bodywork by Alexander and Northern Counties, including some for London. Olympians with Alexander bodies were allocated to companies throughout the Stagecoach empire, with Greater Manchester Buses South getting the biggest batch – 36 – outside of London. The first of an order for 100 low-floor Dennis Tridents were in build at Alexander at the end of the year and were expected to enter service with East London in January 1999.

Small buses were 40 Mercedes-Benz Varios with bodies by Alexander, while new interurban coaches were 20 Volvo B10Ms with Jonckheere Modulo bodies, marking a change from the Plaxton Premieres purchased in previous years. The Modulo is a body not previously seen in the UK.

No major new orders were announced in 1998, other than for 27 MAN double-deck coaches with Jonckheere Monaco bodies for operation on the Oxford Tube.

Older buses in the news were the unusual dual-door Darts which had been favoured by Thames Transit for its Oxford city services. Under Stagecoach ownership 40 of these were moved to London, where two-door buses are more widely accepted.

Stagecoach now operates around 12,000 buses worldwide with 7,300 in Britain.

STAGECOACH GROUP SUBSIDIARIES

Main companies and trading names:

Bayline

Bluebird Buses
  Inverness Traction
  Stagecoach

Burnley & Pendle Transport

Busways Travel Services
  Blue Bus Services
  Magic Bus
  Stagecoach Busways

Cambus Holdings
  Cambus
  Premier Travel Services
  Viscount Bus & Coach Co

Cleveland Transit
  Hartlepool Transport
  Kingston-upon-Hull City Transport
  Stagecoach Darlington
  Stagecoach Hartlepool
  Stagecoach Kingston-upon-Hull
  Stagecoach Transit

Devon General

East London Bus & Coach Co

East Midland Motor Services
  Chesterfield Transport

Eastbourne Bus Company (New Zealand)

Fife Scottish Omnibuses

Greater Manchester Buses South
  Campuslink
  Magic Bus
  Stagecoach Manchester

Grimsby-Cleethorpes Transport Co

Magicbus Scotland (holding co)

National Transport Tokens (99.9%)

Parfitt's Motor Services

PSV Claims Bureau

Rhondda Buses

Ribble Motor Services
  Zippy

Scottish Highway Express

Sistema Metrobus de Bogota (25%)

South East London & Kent Bus Co
  Selkent

Stagecoach Australia

Stagecoach Devon

Stagecoach Glasgow

Stagecoach Graphics

Stagecoach International Services

Stagecoach North West
  Cumberland Motor Services
    Coachlines
    Lakeland Experience
    Stagecoach Lancaster

Stagecoach Portugal (25%)

Stagecoach Scotland

Stagecoach South
  East Kent
  Hampshire Bus
  South Coast Buses
  Stagecoach Hants & Surrey
  Sussex Coastline

Stagecoach Wellington

Stagecoach West
  Aberdare Bus Co
  Cheltenham & Gloucester Omnibus Co
    Gloucester Citybus
    Metro
    Stroud Valleys
  Cheltenham District Traction
    Circle Line
  Midland Red (South)
    G&G Travel
  Red & White Services

Swebus

Swindon & District

Thames Transit
  The Oxford Tube
  Stagecoach Oxford

United Counties Omnibus Co
  Coachlink

The Valleys Bus Co

Wellington City Transport

Western Buses
  AA Buses
  A1 Service

Yellow Bus Co (New Zealand)
  Whenuapai Bus Travel

The Island Line

Porterbrook Leasing

Sheffield Supertram

South West Trains

Virgin Rail (49%)

Most of the double-deckers supplied to Stagecoach in 1998 were long-wheelbase Volvo Olympians with lowheight Alexander R-type bodies. Greater Manchester Buses South received 36. *Peter Rowlands*

Right: Some 50 Dennis Dart SLFs were supplied to Stagecoach for operation in London, all with Alexander ALX200 bodies. This is an East London bus. *SJB*

The first of an order for 150 MANs for Stagecoach entered service in Oxford in the autumn with Thames Transit. The modified livery with a blue roof is part of a route-branding exercise. The MANs have Alexander ALX300 bodies. *Alexander*

STAGECOACH REPRISE – THE MAJOR ACQUISITIONS

1980	Stagecoach formed to run express coach services		*Gray Coach Lines sold*
1985	McLennan, Spittalfield		*Magicbus {Glasgow} sold*
1986	*Magicbus set up in Glasgow*		*Stagecoach Hong Kong set up*
1987	Cumberland Motor Services		*Stagecoach Rail formed*
	Hampshire Bus	1993	East Kent Road Car Co
	Pilgrim Coaches		Grimsby-Cleethorpes
	United Counties		Western Travel
1989	Barrow Borough Transport's operations		Cheltenham & Gloucester
	East Midland Motor Services		Midland Red (South)
	Hastings & District		Red & White
	Inverness Traction		Swindon & District
	Portsmouth City Bus	1994	Busways Travel Services
	Ribble Motor Services		East London Bus & Coach Co
	Bee Line Buzz Co		Cleveland Transit
	Southdown Motor Services		Kingston-upon-Hull
	United Transport Malawi		City Transport
	Perth Panther set up		Hartlepool Transport
1990	Gray Coach Lines, Toronto		Mainline Group (20%)
1991	Fife Scottish Omnibuses		South East London
	Kenya Bus Services (Nairobi)		and Kent Bus Co
	Kenya Bus Services (Mombassa)		Strathclyde Buses (20%)
			Western Scottish Omnibuses
	Northern Scottish Omnibuses		*Stagecoach Darlington set up*
	Portsmouth City Bus sold		*Stagecoach Manchester set up*
1992	Alder Valley (part)	1995	A1 Service
	Lancaster City Transport's operations		Cambus Holdings
	National Transport Tokens		Milton Keynes Citybus
	Wellington City Transport		Viscount
	Cityline Auckland		Chesterfield Transport
	Cityline Hutt Valley		Rodoviaria de Lisboa
			Mainline shareholding sold
			Stagecoach Manchester sold
1996	Burnley & Pendle		
	Transit Holdings (Devon)		
	Bayline		
	Devon General		
	Greater Manchester Buses South		
	Hyndburn Transport		
	Swebus		
	The Island Line		
	Porterbrook Leasing		
	South West Trains		
	Stagecoach Hong Kong ceased		
	Strathclyde Buses shareholding sold		
1997	AA Buses		
	Rhondda Buses		
	Transit Holdings		
	Dockland Transit		
	Thames Transit		
	Transit Australia		
	Stagecoach Glasgow launched		
	Stagecoach Malawi sold		
	Swebus Norge sold		
1998	Yellow Bus, Auckland		
	Sheffield Supertram		
	Virgin Rail (49%)		
	Stagecoach Kenya sold		

New in the South West

DAFs with Plaxton coach bodies are relatively uncommon. Wilts & Dorset took two SB3000s in 1998 with Premiere bodies for use on express services. One leaves Bath for Warminster. *Peter Rowlands*

The first Plaxton Cheetahs were delivered in 1998, with Berkeley Coaches of Paulton being an early customer. The Cheetah is built on the Mercedes-Benz Vario chassis and replaces the Beaver coach. The Beaver continues in production as a bus. *Plaxton*

The Dennis Dart SLF was Britain's best-selling bus in 1998, and most had Plaxton bodies. This is a Super Pointer Dart in Plymouth, one of 14 delivered in the summer. *SJB*

Expocoach 98

THE EXPOCOACH trade show was held at the National Exhibition Centre in October and was used for the launch of some unusual new coaches.

Neoplan used Expocoach for the UK launch of its futuristic Starliner, which is even more striking inside than it is outside. It is powered by a 381bhp 12.8-litre Mercedes engine and has a selling price in the region of £250,000. *SJB*

Pioneer Coaches of Jersey is the first customer for the mid-engined Cannon Hi-line chassis, produced in Northern Ireland and powered by a Cummins B-series engine. It has coachwork by Leicester Carriage Builders. *SJB*

SC Coachcraft of Mexborough – not to be confused with SC Coachbuilders of Waterlooville – showed its Vision at Expocoach, built on a front-engined truck--derived Mercedes-Benz O1120L chassis. The enclosed rear wheelarches have a touch of the 1930s about them, but overall the Vision has to be one of the most successful attempt yet to produce a convincing-looking coach on a chassis of this type. *SJB*

New in the North East and Yorkshire

East Yorkshire bought 15 Volvo Olympians with Northern Counties Palatine I bodies. Six were in fleet livery and nine in the company's pre-1972 deep blue for use on a branded service in Hull. East Yorkshire also bought Northern Counties-bodied Olympians from Eastbourne Buses where they had been displaced by new Optare Spectras. *Plaxton*

New full-sized Mercedes-Benz buses were few and far between outside the West Midlands in 1998. Black Prince of Leeds took two O405s with Optare Prisma bodies. *Michael Fowler*

Smit bodywork re-appeared in the UK after an absence of almost 20 years. The first Smit Stratos, on a DAF SB2750 chassis, was delivered to Fourways Coaches of Leeds in the autumn. The 40-seat Stratos is based on a 10.6m chassis.
Arriva Bus & Coach

The Go-Ahead group bought an interesting variety of buses in 1998 from Volvo, Dennis and Optare. The Dennises were Plaxton-bodied Super Pointer Darts. They are fitted with an automatic vehicle location system which allows Go-Ahead's Gateshead control centre to monitor where each bus is and act to maintain service reliability. *SJB*

Optare's Solo brings the benefit of full accessibility to small buses. The Go-Ahead group took eight for operation in the north-east. the Solo uses the same Mercedes engine as powers the popular Vario minibus, but mounted at the rear. *John Burnett*

The biggest coach operated by Travelgreen of Doncaster is this 8.5m Dennis Javelin with 35-seat Berkhof Excellence 1000 bodywork which entered service in the spring. The 8.5m Javelin is relatively rare – most Javelins are 12m long. The Berkhof Excellence body was phased out during 1998, being replaced by the Axial and the Radial. *Dennis*

Consolidation in the capital

NEW BUSES CONTINUED to appear on the streets of London in large numbers during 1998, and these ranged from the last Dennis Arrows (for Capital Citybus) to the first of the new generation of low-floor DAF double-deckers, for Arriva London North. New operators appeared on tendered services, and there were some changes among established businesses, most notably the acquisition by FirstGroup of London's biggest independent, Capital Citybus, the take-over of MTL London Northern by neighbouring Metroline, and the collapse of Q Drive, owners of Limebourne.

The year started with a number of tendered services changing hands. In January Tellings Golden Miller gained the 235, Sunbury to Brentford, from London United, buying 14 Dennis Dart SLFs with Plaxton bodies to operate it. Harris Bus won routes in the south-east from both Kentish Bus and Selkent, and expanded its fleet with new Volvo Olympians with East Lancs bodies. Similar vehicles were bought by Metrobus for a route it won from Kentish Bus. Indeed, Kentish Bus fared rather badly at the start of the year and the loss of contracts to Harris Bus and Metrobus led to the closure of the company's Cambridge Heath operating base and the transfer of 48 buses, mainly Northern Counties-bodied Leyland Olympians, to sister Arriva company Leaside.

London General lost the high-profile C1 minibus service linking Victoria and Kensington. The contract was awarded to a new operator, Travel London, but from February to June it was run jointly by Metrobus and Selkent. Selkent provided Mercedes Varios; Metrobus used Optare MetroRiders. When Travel London took over it initially used ten new Wright-bodied Volvo B6LEs, on loan from Travel West Midlands, a sister company within the National Express Group. These were later replaced by London's first Optare Solos. Travel London also won the 211, Waterloo to Hammersmith, from London General, taking it over in June, and for this bought 21 stylish Optare Excels.

Prior to selling out to FirstGroup, Capital Citybus had been having some success with its tender bids, and during the year it bought 28 Dennis Arrows and 17 Volvo Olympians to cover new routes, as well as a batch of Darts. Its profile in central London was raised when it took on the 76 and the 259 (from Leaside) in March and the 341 from Arriva London North in the autumn.

Capital Citybus was London's biggest independent operator with 300 buses when it was bought by FirstGroup in July. The takeover saw some rationalisation of FirstGroup's interests in the capital, with Capital Citybus taking over two routes and 14 buses, the D8 and W9, from Thamesway in the summer, followed by the 48-bus Ponders End depot in September.

The other Capital, Capital Logistics, made the news for a variety of reasons. In May it took over the U3, Uxbridge to

Seen immediately before entering service at the start of November, this Alexander ALX400 on a DAF chassis heralds the start of a new generation of fully-accessible London double-deckers. *Alexander*

Heathrow, from CentreWest, using a fleet of Optare Excels with the luxury of air-conditioning for the first time on an ordinary London bus service. It also took over operation of the 726 from Dartford to Heathrow from London Coaches, and the Ikarus-bodied DAFs which operated it. Then it announced the first order for low-floor double-deckers to be placed by a London independent. This was for 16 DAFs, ten Plaxton Presidents and six Optare Spectras. The original President specification included air-conditioning and double-glazing, although a re-think saw these being dropped.

These were for route 60 in the Croydon area, which was due to be taken over by Capital Logistics in August. In the event Selkent and Blue Triangle started running it on Capital Logistics' behalf, and then Capital Logistics pulled out, with an announcement from LT in November that new operator Omnibus London would be taking the 16 DAFs and running the contract. At the end of the year the 60 was still being covered by Selkent and Blue Triangle.

There was consolidation in north London in August when Metroline bought the neighbouring MTL London operation. Metroline ran some 450 buses; MTL London had around 400. MTL had bought London Northern in 1994, renaming it MTL London Northern and then simply MTL London. It expanded in 1995 by buying London Suburban and R&I Coaches, both of which operated LT tendered services. The all-over red MTL London livery was quickly amended by Metroline to include a blue skirt – the standard Metroline colour scheme – and the operation was renamed Metroline London Northern.

The collapse of Q Drive in the autumn put Limebourne in the spotlight so far as London bus operations were concerned. Limebourne had 31 buses-including 19 low-floor Dennis Darts – on four LT routes, the C3, C10, 42 and 156. The operation was bought by its management and a new company, Independent Way, was formed. But most of the fleet

was repossessed by the finance companies which had supplied it, leaving Independent Way to cover operations with a selection of hired buses until replacements could be acquired.

In December London Sovereign put eight new Northern Counties-bodied Olympians into operation on the 292, replacing Metroline Metrobuses.

While Olympians were the most common double-deck type to be delivered to London operators in 1998 – other buyers included Harris Bus, Metrobus, Metroline, Go-Ahead and Stagecoach – the most interesting were the first low-floor models. The very first, an Arriva DAF with Alexander ALX400 body was launched in May, but it wasn't until November that Arriva's new fleet of DAFs started entering service on the 242 from Tottenham Court Road to Homerton Hospital.

By the end of the year there were around a couple of dozen in

service, but the number will grow rapidly in 1999 as low-floor 'deckers become the London standard. Orders were placed during 1998 by FirstGroup, Go-Ahead, Metroline and Stagecoach, all joining Arriva in spreading the low-floor message. The new ALX400s are attractive buses, but the adoption of a low floor in a two-door bus imposes severe constraints on lower-deck seating with Arriva's DAFs having just 17 seats in the lower saloon.

However high-floor buses have some way to go yet. A batch of Northern Counties-bodied Volvo Olympians to London specification were being built for the manufacturers' stock at the end of 1998. And lest anyone fear that all this activity means the end of the Routemaster, LT tenders awarded in 1998 suggest that the trusty Routemaster should survive until 2003. Some were still being fitted with new Scania engines during 1998.

MAJOR CHANGES IN TENDERED ROUTES 1998		
1	Tottenham Court Road - Rotherhithe	London Central to First Capital
60	Old Coulsdon - Streatham Common	Arriva London South to Capital Logistics
76	County Hall - Northumberland Park	Leaside to Capital Citybus
119	Bromley - Croydon Airport	Selkent to Metrobus
127	Purley - Tooting	Arriva Croydon & North Surrey to London General/Selkent
132	Eltham Station - Bexleyheath	Kentish Bus to Harris Bus
180	Thamesmead - Lewisham	Selkent to Harris Bus
210	Finsbury Park - Brent Cross	Grey - Green to Thorpe
211	Waterloo - Hammersmith	London General to Travel London
214	Liverpool Street - Highgate	Thamesway to MTL London
225	Lewisham - Bermondsey	Arriva London North East to Selkent
233	Swanley - Eltham Station	Kentish Bus to Metrobus
237	Shepherds Bush - Hounslow Heath	London United to Armchair
243	Wood Green - Holborn Circus	Thamesway to MTL London
259	Edmonton Green - King's Cross	Leaside to Capital Citybus
260	Shepherds Bush - North Finchley	Armchair to Metroline
272	Woolwich - Abbeywood Circular	Arriva Kent Thameside to Selkent
292	Borehamwood - Colindale	Metroline to London Sovereign
320	Bromley North - Westerham	Selkent to Metrobus
341	County Hall - Northumberland Park	Arriva London North to Capital Citybus
404	Coulsdon - Caterham on the Hill	Metrobus to Epsom Buses
726	Dartford - Heathrow	London Coaches to Capital Logistics
C1	Victoria - Kensington	London General to Travel London
D8	Stratford - Crossharbour	Thamesway to Capital Citybus
S2	Stratford - Clapton	East London to Capital Citybus
U3	Uxbridge - Heathrow	CentreWest to Capital Logistics
U9	Uxbridge - Harefield Hospital	CentreWest to Arriva The Shires
W8	Chase Farm Hospital - Lea Valley	MTL London to Capital Citybus
W9	Chase Farm Hospital - Southgate Station	Thamesway to Capital Citybus

Prior to taking delivery of new Optare Solos, Travel London started running the C1 using Volvo B6LEs borrowed from Travel West Midlands. They had Wright Crusader bodies. *SJB*

Thorpe, best-known for running the Stationlink service, expanded in the autumn when it took over the operation of the 210, a one-time Grey-Green route. For this it ordered 12 Plaxton-bodied Dennis Darts. *Plaxton*

An unusual type to find in London service is the East Lancs Spryte. Capital Citybus has 13 on Dennis Dart SLF chassis, bought early in the year for use on the S2. *SJB*

London Traveller operates a number of school services for LT and in 1998 bought a new double decker: a Dennis Arrow with East Lancs Pyoneer body. It was unusual in being fitted with coach seats with belts. *SJB*

Above, right: MTL London took delivery of a large number of Dennis Darts with Marshall Capital bodies shortly before being taken over by Metroline. A Dart passes through Trafalgar Square before the MTL sale. *SJB*

Perhaps the most impressive new fleet in London in 1998 was the Volvo/Northern Counties combination delivered to London General. There were 25 of these Palatine IIs finished to a high specification which included coach-style seating. *Peter Rowlands*

Travel London was a new name to appear the capital in the summer, taking over two routes from London General. One was operated by 21 new Optare Excels. *SJB*

New in the Midlands & East Anglia

Zak's – the nickname of owner Kevin Fazakarley – added five new Mercedes-Benz Varios to its fleet in 1998, unusual for a small operator in having automatic gearboxes. They had Plaxton Beaver 2 bodies. *Plaxton*

Travel West Midlands took large numbers of Wright Crusader bodies in 1998. Most were on Volvo B6LEs, but four were also purchased on Dennis Dart SLF chassis. The Darts were allocated to Travel Your Bus. *Wright*

Caetano's Enigma, launched in 1997, received a minor facelift before production models were delivered during 1998. Commandery Coaches of Worcester took this Enigma on a Dennis Javelin chassis. *Dennis*

Few Optare Deltas entered service in 1998 as more operators switch to later flat-floor models. Sanders of Holt took two, on DAF SB220 chassis. *Geoff Mills*

The first double-deckers for Cambridge Coach Services were two Volvo Olympians with Northern Counties bodies. They are used on coastal services. *Geoff Mills*

The only Scania double-decker to enter service in 1998 did so with Fowlers of Holbeach. It is an N113 with an East Lancs Cityzen body. It is seen here immediately before entering service on 1 August. *Geoff Mills*

FirstGroup looks east

THE MAJOR NEWS for FirstGroup was not in Britain, but in the Far East. In a joint venture with New World Development of Hong Kong, FirstGroup won the race to take over the 700-bus, 88-route franchise previously held by China Motor Bus. A new company, New World First Bus, was set up and, no doubt to the delight of British manufacturers, quickly ordered almost 250 new buses.

But back home there was some expansion too. Halesworth Transit,

better known by its trading name, Flying Banana, operated 15 minibuses in Great Yarmouth, and was taken over by Eastern Counties in May. The company had been operating in the town since 1989. April also saw the merger of FirstGroup's two businesses in South Wales: Brewers and South Wales Transport in an expanded SWT, although retaining the Brewers trading name. A rather smaller change was the end of Hants &

Sussex in May, absorbed into the Southampton City Transport business which had taken it over in May 1996.

The following month FirstGroup took control of Mainline, running some 800 buses in South Yorkshire. It had held a 20 per cent stake in Mainline since the end of 1995. Mainline was the successor to the South Yorkshire PTE's bus operation and had been privatised in a management-led employee buy-out in 1993.

New World First Bus took delivery of Dennis Tridents and Darts. A Trident with Alexander ALX500 body is seen at First Aberdeen's centenary celebrations. *SJB*

FirstGroup put Italian built electric buses, left-hand-drive Tecnobus Gullivers, into service with Bristol City Line and PMT. Bristol had two for use on a park-and-ride service in the city centre. *SJB*

Mainline had in May taken over the Northern Bus operation, in which it already had a minority shareholding. It retained 17 of the Northern Bus vehicles. With FirstGroup already owning the former West Yorkshire PTE operations in the shape of the Rider Group, it was now firmly established as the major bus operator in the Yorkshire area.

Modest expansion in York saw Glenn Line give up local bus operations, with First York taking over in June and acquiring seven Leyland Nationals in the process.

In July FirstGroup bought London's biggest independent bus company, Capital Citybus, along with the associated Walthamstow Citybus which also traded under the Capital name. Capital Citybus operated 300 buses. Prior to a management buy-out in December 1995 the company had been owned by Hong Kong City Bus (from December 1990) - and before that had been the operating arm of Ensign Bus, the long-established Essex-based bus dealer.

Some 18 months of uncertainty in central Scotland came to an end in July when it was announced that an appeal by FirstGroup against a Monopolies & Mergers Commission ruling had been successful. At the start of 1997, while the Conservatives were still in power, the MMC had said that FirstGroup had to sell Midland Bluebird and one of the Glasgow depots of Strathclyde Buses because it was feared that FirstGroup's acquisition of Strathclyde and the subsidiary Kelvin Central business gave it too strong a position in the region.

However with Labour's interest in promoting integration it would have been surprising if the MMC ruling had been upheld. The

Northern Bus was taken over by Mainline, whose fleetname is just visible on the first nearside window of this acquired Leyland National at Meadowhall. *SJB*

New buses which are not to FirstGroup specification do not receive the group's corporate colours. Mainline had ordered Super Pointer Darts at the end of 1997 and although they were delivered after the FirstGroup takeover they carried Mainline colours. *SJB*

successful appeal means that FirstGroup remains the main operator of buses in a region stretching across central Scotland from Dumbarton in the west, through Stirling in the north right down to the English border on the east coast. Services in Edinburgh are shared between FirstGroup and Lothian Region Transport.

In October FirstGroup took over part of the Timeline bus operation in Greater Manchester, along with 51 fairly modern buses including six Volvo B10Ls and ten Optare Excels. It further consolidated its position in the region by acquiring the bus operations of Pioneer of Rochdale in November, with 12 vehicles.

While FirstGroup is a young organisation it does have a considerable transport heritage, and this was celebrated in Aberdeen in the summer with a weekend to mark the centenary of the city's public transport. Aberdeen Corporation first operated trams in 1898 and from there became a bus operator in 1920, was taken over by Grampian Regional Transport in 1975 which in turn was bought by its employees in 1989. The privatised GRT group expanded and merged with Badgerline in 1995 to create FirstBus, now FirstGroup.

The centenary event attracted preserved buses from around the country which underlined just how extensive FirstGroup's roots are – from a preserved Western National Bristol VRT to a Leeds Corporation AEC Regent. Aberdeen's own transport history was ably covered by a 1930 Albion, along with a 1965 Daimler CVG6, a couple of AEC Swifts and a 1975 Leyland Leopard, as well as a range of former Alexander (Northern) buses representing the other major operator in the north-east of Scotland, which is now part of the Stagecoach group.

A rather more modest celebration marked the end of 40 years of Atlantean operation in Glasgow. In June a special service was operated using the preserved original Glasgow Corporation Atlantean, along with specially

repainted later vehicles. However Atlantean operation continued after this date, with the final example coming out of service with First Glasgow in October. There had been a plan to preserve Glasgow's last Atlantean – but it was scrapped by mistake.

New buses for FirstGroup in 1998 included over 300 low-floor single-deckers with Wright bodywork. Although outwardly similar, around a third were on Volvo B10BLE chassis (the biggest users being First Manchester and Mainline), with others on Scania L113 and, later in the year, a few on the new Scania L94UB. Other single-deckers were mainly Dennis Dart SLFs with Plaxton Pointer 2 bodies. of which there were some 250. Most new single-deckers were in corporate colours, but 31 Darts for Mainline – of which 20 had been ordered by Mainline and 11 by Northern Bus – were delivered in Mainline livery. Over 100 Dart SLFs with Marshall bodies were supplied to CentreWest and Bee Line.

Small buses were Plaxton-bodied Mercedes and, for Quickstep in Leeds, half-a-dozen Optare Solos. The low-floor Solos were in FirstGroup corporate colours while the high-floor Mercs were in the individual liveries of the fleets receiving them. The biggest batch of small buses comprised 64 Mercedes for Midland Red West, where they replaced first-generation minibuses on services in Worcester. In all, Plaxton supplied over 100 Beaver 2s on Mercedes, while a small batch of Marshall-bodied Mercedes went to the group's Essex Buses operation.

Double-deckers – around 100 in total – were all Volvo Olympians and, underlining FirstGroup's commitment to making public transport attractive, had Alexander Royale or Northern Counties Palatine II bodies, rather than the more basic R-type or Palatine I. The only fleets receiving new double-deckers in 1998 were Lowland, Midland Bluebird, Bristol Cityline, First Manchester and Yorkshire Rider.

The Bristol buses had Northern Counties bodies; the other fleets had Alexander bodies. In addition Capital Citybus received a batch of Olympians with Palatine I bodies which had been ordered before the company had sold out to FirstGroup. These had FirstGroup-style interiors.

The most unusual new buses for FirstGroup – indeed for any British operator in 1998 – were Italian-built Tecnobuses. Two entered service with Bristol Cityline in July, and six more followed in the Wirral area in the autumn with PMT. The diminutive Tecnobuses are battery-powered and left-hand-drive. They seat just nine people – with no allowance for standees because of their high weight: 4080kg unladen.

Another alternative to diesel power was evaluated by PMT with the purchase of a DAF SB220 powered by LPG. It entered service with Crosville in Chester in the spring.

While Arriva went in for wholesale re-naming of its companies, only a few FirstGroup subsidiaries adopted new company names in 1998. These started in April with First Aberdeen (formerly Grampian Transport) followed in May by First Manchester (previously Greater Manchester Buses North). Also in May, Strathclyde Buses became First Glasgow (No1) while Kelvin Central became First Glasgow (No2). Both businesses adopted the First Glasgow trading name, except in Ayrshire where what had been First Kelvin became First Ayrshire. In November the Eastern Counties Omnibus Co became First Eastern Counties Buses

Underlining its emphasis on quality, FirstGroup launched TwinTrack in 1998, a plan to improve bus service quality in which investment by FirstGroup would be matched by investment by government. Under the plans – if they actually proceed – 465 extra new buses would enter service in Greater Manchester and West Yorkshire over the next three years.

FirstGroup operates almost 9,000 buses in Britain.

Crowds turned out to watch a parade marking 100 years of public transport in Aberdeen. A preserved Aberdeen Corporation Albion led a line-up of 100 buses old and new. *SJB*

Double-deckers played a relatively small part in FirstGroup's new vehicle purchases in 1998. Bristol City Line took 26 Volvo Olympians with Northern Counties bodies. *SJB*

FIRSTGROUP

Bristol Omnibus Co
   Badgerline
   City Line
   Durbin
   Streamline
Berks Bucks Bus Company
   Bee Line
Capital Citybus
CentreWest London Buses
   Challenger
   Ealing Buses
   Heathrow Fast
   London Buslines
   Orpington Buses
   Uxbridge Buses
Essex Buses
   Eastern National
   Thamesway
First Aberdeen
First Eastern Counties
   Blue Bus
   Halesworth Transit
     Flying Banana
   Rosemary Coaches
First Glasgow (No1)
First Glasgow (No2)
   First Ayrshire
First Manchester

First Pioneer
Kirkpatrick of Deeside
Leicester Citybus
Lowland Omnibuses
   Ian Glass Coaches
   Lothian Transit
   SMT
Mainline Group
   Don Valley Buses
   First Mainline
Mairs of Aberdeen
Midland Bluebird
   Fife First
   Kings of Dunblane
   SMT
Midland Red West
   Citibus
Northampton Transport
PMT
   Crosville
   First Pennine
   Red Rider
Provincial
Rider York
South Wales Transport
   Brewers
Southampton Citybus
Wessex Coaches

Sky Blue
Western National
   Roberts
Yorkshire Rider
   First Bradford
   First Calderline
   First Huddersfield
   First Superbus
   Quickstep Travel

North West Trains
Great Eastern Railways
Great Western Trains*

* minority shareholding

FirstGroup took delivery of over 250 Dennis Darts with Plaxton Pointer 2 bodies. These included ten of the new 11.3m-long Super Pointer Dart, five of which were allocated to the group's Yorkshire operations. *Plaxton*

New Mercedes-Benz Varios for FirstGroup carried company liveries, as shown by a Midland Red West bus in Worcester. It has Plaxton Beaver 2 bodywork. *SJB*

Wright supplied over 250 buses to FirstGroup in 1998. First Manchester took almost 50 Renowns on Volvo B10BLE chassis. *Peter Rowlands*

Q Drive folds

THE SUDDEN COLLAPSE of Q Drive in October signalled the end for an operation which grew out of London Buslines, set up by Len Wright in 1985 to operate a London Transport contracted route between Hounslow and Slough using second-hand Fleetlines – bought from LT. Len Wright was previously best-known as an operator of purpose-designed high-specification coaches for transporting pop groups. London Buslines started in July 1985 and soon won additional tenders for which it bought new Leyland Lynxes and Olympians.

Q Drive was formed as a holding company in 1987 and in December of that year bought the Berks Bucks Bus Company – formerly Alder Valley North – from the National Bus Company. This traded as the Bee Line.

Q Drive added Alder Valley South at the end of 1988, thus re-uniting the company which had been split in 1986 in preparation for privatisation. The "South" was dropped from the Alder Valley name. Q Drive also bought Alder Valley Engineering, which expanded into coach dealing with a Berkhof franchise, trading as AVE Berkhof.

The first cut-backs came at the end of 1990. When the Bee Line operations in High Wycombe with 51 buses were sold to City of Oxford and rebranded as the Wycombe Bus Company. Then in December London & Country (at that time part of the Drawlane organisation) took over Alder Valley's operations in and around Guildford, with 50 vehicles.

Restructuring in 1992 saw further contraction. The Bee Line business in Reading and Newbury was sold to Reading Transport in August, along with 56 vehicles. Reading had earlier, in September 1991, taken over the Bee Line's Reading to London commuter operations. In October 1992 the remainder of the Alder Valley business with 90 buses serving was sold to Stagecoach, becoming Stagecoach Hants & Surrey.

All that remained of the Bee Line were the operations in Maidenhead and Bracknell. In the space of 12 months Q Drive's fleet was halved, from 300 to 150 vehicles.

Then came brief expansion, with the takeover in February 1993 of the Slough operations of London Country North West, which added 40 buses to what was now known as Q Drive Buses, which had taken over both the Bee Line and London Buslines, although both were retained as trading names.

In June 1995 Q Drive bought London-based Limebourne Coaches, which ran 24 vehicles. This was but a prelude to bigger changes – the sale in March 1996 of all of Q Drive's bus operations to CentreWest, extending the then independent London operator's territory westwards into Berkshire while consolidating its position in west and north-west London, the location of most of London Buslines' routes. CentreWest acquired 180 buses from Q Drive.

This left Q Drive running Limebourne Coaches and AVE Berkhof. The company's coaching interests expanded in 1996 with the acquisition of the 43-vehicle Scancoaches business in London, and up-market coach touring holidays were launched by a new subsidiary, Cirrus Travel, trading as The Glider. Q Drive also took over the operations of Eurobus, running scheduled services to mainland Europe.

The company re-appeared as a bus operator in a small way in 1996 when Limebourne took over a London Transport tendered service, running Optare MetroRiders on the C10 to the Elephant & Castle. It won two further routes in 1997, for which it bought Dennis Dart SLFs with Plaxton bodies.

And then it crashed. In October Q Drive called in the receivers.

There followed weeks of hectic activity as the receivers tried to sell the various parts of Q Drive as going concerns – and coach dealers sweated at the thought of the modern Q Drive fleet appearing on an already over-stocked second-hand market.

It quickly became clear that Berkhof was not going to be without a UK distributor. Some of the assets of AVE Berkhof were bought by the Dutch manufacturer and a new company was formed in November: Berkhof UK. A new company, Independent Way, was set up by the Limebourne management working with the company's previous owner from whom Q Drive had purchased the business in 1995. However Limebourne's buses, which were leased, were repossessed leaving the new owners to run services with a collection of hired vehicles.

Scan Coaches was bought by Driver Express – but the name was immediately re-sold to Stort Valley Coaches, one of London's fastest-growing coach businesses.

And that was the end of Q Drive.

An assortment of vehicles appeared on former Limebourne services after Independent Way took over. These included ex-Metroline Darts and, as here, ex-Grey-Green Volvos, all still in their previous owners' colours. *SJB*

Who makes what?

A guide to chassis available to UK operators in 1998, or announced in 1998 with availability for 1999.

Make and model	Engine Position	Overall Length (m)	Wheel base (m)	Engine	Cubic Capacity (l)	Power (bhp)	Gearbox	Speeds
AYATS integral (Spain)								
Atlas	RV	12.0	-	Various	-	-	-	-
Bravo II	RV	12.0	-	Various	-	-	-	-
Bravo I dd	RV	12.0	-	Various	-	-	-	-
Offered with the choice of Cummins, MAN and Mercedes engines in the 340-460bhp range and with ZF manual or automatic gearboxes.								
BOVA integral (Holland)								
Futura FHD12-340	RV	12.0	6.09	DAF WS242	11.6	329	ZF S6-85	6 M
Futura FHD12-330L	RV	12.0	6.09	DAF RS200	8.66	333	ZF S6-85	6 M
Futura FHC12-300	RV	12.0	6.09	Cummins C	8.3	300	ZF S6-85	6 M
Futura Club FLC	RV	12.0	6.09	Cummins C	8.3	275	ZF S6-85	6 M
Futura Club FLD	RV	12.0	6.09	DAF RS245M	8.66	388	ZF S6-85	6 M
Futura FHD10-340	RV	10.0	4.89	DAF WS242	11.6	329	ZF S6-85	6 M
DAF (Holland)								
DB250	RV	9.9	5.05	DAF RS200	8.65	272	Voith D851.3	3 A
DB250LF	RV	10.4	5.45	DAF RS200	8.65	272	Voith D851.3	3 A
Gearbox options – ZF 5HP500, Voith D854.3								
SB220	RH	11.6	5.50	DAF LT160L	11.6	218	ZF 4HP500	4 A
SB220 GS	RH	11.9	5.50	DAF GS160	8.65	218	ZF 4HP500	4 A
SB220ULF	RH	11.5	6.00	DAF GS160	8.65	218	ZF 4HP500	4 A
SB220GG	RH	11.6	6.00	DAF GG 170 LPG	8.65	231	ZF 4HP500	4 A
Gearbox options – ZF 5HP500, Voith D851.3, Voith D854.3								
SB3000WS	RV	11.9	6.02	DAF WS242	11.6	330	ZF 8S-140	8 M
DENNIS (UK)								
Dart	RV	8.5	3.78	Cummins B	5.9	130	Allison AT545	4 A
Dart	RV	9.0	4.30	Cummins B	5.9	130	Allison AT545	4 A
Dart	RV	9.8	5.12	Cummins B	5.9	130	Allison AT545	4 A
Dart SLF	RV	8.8	3.90	Cummins B	5.9	130	Allison AT545	4 A
Dart SLF	RV	9.0	4.40	Cummins B	5.9	130	Allison AT545	4 A
Dart SLF	RV	10.0	5.20	Cummins B	5.9	130	Allison AT545	4 A
Dart SLF	RV	10.5	5.81	Cummins B	5.9	145	Allison AT545	4 A
Super Pointer Dart	RV	11.3	5.95	Cummins B	5.9	160	Allison B300R	4 A
Javelin	UV	8.5	4.00	Cummins C	8.3	211	ZF S6-85	6 M
Javelin	UV	10.0	5.00	Cummins C	8.3	245	ZF S6-85	6 M
Javelin	UV	12.0	6.25	Cummins C	8.3	245	ZF S6-85	6 M
Javelin GX	UV	12.0	6.25	Cummins C	8.3	300	ZF S6-85	6 M
Arrow	RV	10.5	5.05	Cummins C	8.3	245	ZF 4HP500	4 A
Trident	RV	9.9	5.25	Cummins C	8.3	220	ZF 4HP500	4 A
Trident	RV	10.5	5.80	Cummins C	8.3	220	ZF 4HP500	4 A
Trident engine option – 245bhp, gearbox options – ZF 5HP500, Voith D851								
IVECO (Italy/Spain)								
DailyBus 49.10	FV	6.36	3.60	Iveco 8140.27S	2.5	104	Iveco 2826	5 M
DailyBus 49.10	FV	6.76	3.95	Iveco 8140.27S	2.5	104	Iveco 2826	5 M
DailyBus 59.12	FV	7.04	4.18	Iveco 8140.47S	2.5	116	Iveco 2826	5 M
DailyBus 59.12	FV	7.64	4.48	Iveco 8140.47S	2.5	116	Iveco 2826	5 M
EuroMidi	FV	9.73	4.63	Iveco 8060.45B	5.86	177	Iveco 2855.6	6 M
EuroRider 29	RV	12.0	6.15	Iveco 8640.41R	9.5	290	ZF S6-85	6 M
EuroRider 35	RV	12.0	6.15	Iveco 8640.41T	9.5	345	ZF 8S-180	8 M
EuroRider Interurban	RV	12.0	6.15	Iveco 8640.41R	9.5	290	ZF 5HP600	5 A
KASSBOHRER integral (Germany)								
Setra S250	RV	12.0	6.08	Mercedes OM442LA	15.1	381	ZF 8S-180	8 M
Setra S250	RV	12.0	6.08	Mercedes OM442LA	15.1	381	Allison	6 A
Setra S250	RV	12.0	6.08	MAN D2866	11.9	370	ZF 8S-180	8 M
MAN (Germany)								
11.220 bus	RV	10.0	4.9	MAN D0826	6.9	220	ZF 4HP500	4 A
11.220 coach	RV	9.0	-	MAN D0828	6.9	220	ZF S6-36	6 M
13.220 bus	RV	10.0	4.7	MAN D0826	6.9	220	ZF 4HP500	4 A
NL222F	RH	11.7	5.8	MAN D0826	6.9	220	Voith D851.3	3 A
18.220 bus	RV	12.0	-	MAN D0826	6.9	220	Voith D851.3	3 A
18.310	RV	12.0	-	MAN D2866	12.0	310	ZF S6-85	6 M
24.400	RV	12.0	-	MAN D2866	12.0	400	ZF 8S-180	8 M

34

MARSHALL integral (UK)

Model	Pos			Engine	Litres	bhp	Gearbox	Speeds
Minibus	RV	8.5	3.94	Cummins B	3.9	135	Allison AT545	4 A
Minibus	RV	8.5	3.94	Perkins Phaser	4.0	135	Allison AT545	4 A

MERCEDES-BENZ (Germany)

Model	Pos			Engine	Litres	bhp	Gearbox	Speeds
Vario O-814D	FV	6.94	4.25	Mercedes OM904LA	4.25	136	ZF 5S-42	5 M
Vario O-814D	FV	7.49	4.80	Mercedes OM904LA	4.25	136	ZF 5S-42	5 M
Gearbox option – Allison AT542 automatic								
O1120L	FV	9.15	4.84	Mercedes OM366LA	5.96	211	Mercedes G4	6 M
O404 Vita	RV	12.0	6.25	Mercedes OM441LA	10.96	340	Mercedes GO4	6 M
O405	RH	11.6	5.88	Mercedes OM447H	11.97	213	ZF 4HP500	4 A
O405N	RH	12.0	5.88	Mercedes OM447H	11.97	213	ZF 4HP500	4 A

NEOPLAN integral (Germany)

Model	Pos			Engine	Litres	bhp	Gearbox	Speeds
N4014	RH	12.0	6.02	MAN D2866	11.9	230	ZF 5HP500	5 A
Jetliner N212H	RV	9.85	4.75	Mercedes OM401LA	9.6	290	ZF S6-1600	6 M
Cityliner N116/2	RV	12.0	6.10	Mercedes OM441LA	10.96	340	ZF S6-1600	6 M
Cityliner N116/3	RV	12.0	5.45	Mercedes OM442LA	11.9	381	ZF 8S-1600	8 M
Cityliner N116/3	RV	12.0	5.45	Scania DSC11-70	11.0	381	Scania GR801	7 M
Skyliner N122/3 dd	RV	12.0	5.55	Mercedes OM402LA	12.8	381	ZF 8S-1600	8 M
Skyliner N122/3 dd	RV	12.0	5.55	MAN D2866	11.9	370	ZF 8S-1600	8 M
Starliner N516SHD	RV	12.0	5.55	Mercedes OM402LA	12.8	381	ZF 8S-1600	8 M

OPTARE integral (UK)

Model	Pos			Engine	Litres	bhp	Gearbox	Speeds
MetroRider 4	FV	7.7	4.75	Cummins B	5.9	130	Allison AT545	4 A
MetroRider 4	FV	8.5	4.75	Cummins B	5.9	130	Allison AT545	4 A
Solo M850	RV	8.5	5.53	Mercedes OM904LA	4.25	122	Allison AT545	4 A
Solo M920	RV	9.2	6.23	Mercedes OM904LA	4.25	122	Allison AT545	4 A
Excel L960	RV	9.6	4.23	Cummins B	5.9	160	Allison B300R	4 A
Excel L1000	RV	10.0	4.66	Cummins B	5.9	160	Allison B300R	4 A
Excel L1070	RV	10.7	5.37	Cummins B	5.9	160	Allison B300R	4 A
Excel L1150	RV	11.5	6.09	Cummins B	5.9	160	Allison B300R	4 A

SCANIA (Sweden)

Model	Pos			Engine	Litres	bhp	Gearbox	Speeds
L113CRL	RV	11.7	5.90	Scania DSC11	11.0	260	ZF 4HP600	4 A
N113DRB	RV	9.5	4.95	Scania DS11	11.0	220	Voith D863	3 A
N113DRB	RV	10.18	5.64	Scania DS11	11.0	220	Voith D863	3 A
K93CRB	RV	12.0	-	Scania DSC09	9.0	283	Scania GR801/CS	7 M
K113CRB	RV	12.0	-	Scania DSC11	11.0	340	Scania GR801/CS	7 M
K113TRB	RV	12.0	-	Scania DSC11	11.0	362	Scania GR801/CS	7 M
K124IB	RV	12.0	6.0	Scania DSC12-02	12.0	360	Scania GR801/CS	7 M
L94 Axcess Floline	RV	11.8	6.0	Scania DSC9-11	9.0	220	ZF 4HP500	4 A
L94IB	RV	12.0	5.82	Scania DSC9-15	9.0	310	Scania GR801/CS	7 M
L94IB	RV	12.0	5.82	Scania DSC9-15	9.0	310	ZF 5HP600	5 A

VAN HOOL integral (Belgium)

Model	Pos			Engine	Litres	bhp	Gearbox	Speeds
EOS 80	RV	9.5	4.49	Mercedes OM411LA	10.9	290	ZF S6-85	6 M
EOS 90	RV	12.0	5.95	MAN D2866	11.9	311	ZF 6S-1600	6 M
EOS90	RV	12.0	5.95	MAN D2866	11.9	311	ZF 5HP590	5 A
EOS230	RV	12.0	5.8	MAN D2866	11.9	400	ZF 6S-1600	6 M

VOLVO (Sweden/UK)

Model	Pos			Engine	Litres	bhp	Gearbox	Speeds
Olympian	RV	9.6	4.95	Volvo D10A	9.6	245	ZF 4HP500	4 A
Olympian	RV	10.3	5.64	Volvo D10A	9.6	245	ZF 4HP500	4 A
Gearbox options – ZF 5HP500, Voith D863								
B7L	RV	9.9	-	Volvo D7C	6.7	210	ZF 4HP500	4 A
B7L	RV	10.4	-	Volvo D7C	6.7	210	ZF 4HP500	4 A
Engine options – 250, 290 bhp ratings. Gearbox option – Voith								
B6LE	RV	10.6	5.32	Volvo D6A	5.48	180	ZF 4HP500	4 A
B6BLE	RV	10.5	5.32	Volvo D6A	5.48	180	ZF 4HP500	4 A
Engine option – 210bhp rating								
B7R	RV	12.0	6.30	Volvo D7B	6.7	260	ZF S6-85	6 M
Gearbox option – ZF 4HP500								
B10B	RH	11.5	5.80	Volvo DH10A	9.6	245	ZF 4HP 500	4 A
B10BLE	RH	12.0	-	Volvo DH10A	9.6	245	ZF 5HP500	5 A
B10L	RH	12.0	-	Volvo DH10A	9.6	245	ZF 5HP500	5 A
B10L	RH	12.0	-	Volvo GH10A CNG	9.6	245	ZF 5HP500	5 A
B10M Citybus	UH	10.0	5.50	Volvo DH10A	9.6	245	ZF 4HP500	4 A
B9M	UH	10.0	4.80	Volvo DH10A	9.6	245	ZF S6-85	5 M
B10M GL	UH	12.0	6.20	Volvo DH10A	9.6	285	ZF S6-85	6 M
B10M GLE	UH	12.0	6.20	Volvo DH10A	9.6	360	Volvo G8 EGS	8 M
B10M SE	UH	12.0	4.80	Volvo DH10A	9.6	285	ZF 5HP590	5 A
B10MT	UH	12.0	5.20	Volvo DH10A	9.6	360	Volvo G8 EGS	8 M
B12T	RV	12.0	6.10	Volvo D12A	12.1	420	Volvo G8 EGS	8 M
Engine options – 340 and 380bhp ratings								

Codes: Engine position – **F** Front, **U** Underfloor, **R** Rear, **H** Horizontal, **V** Vertical ; Gearbox – number indicates forward speeds, **A** Automatic, **M** Manual

1998 Roundup

January

• Canadian bus manufacturer Prevost, owned jointly by Henlys and Volvo, buys NovaBus.

• The Strathclyde PTE announces that three electric Omnis, modified by Smiths Electric Vehicles, will be running in Glasgow in the spring. Although delivered, they are still not in use by the end of the year.

• Cawlett, owners of Southern National, buy Smiths Coaches of Portland (17 vehicles). The name is to be retained. Cawlett had previously owned Smiths between 1990 and 1994.

• FTL Omni relaunches the Omni low-floor minibus with plans to build 30 in 1998. It now has an Iveco engine in place of the previous Perkins unit. FTL Omni took over production from previous builders, the Omni Coach Co, in 1997.

• FastTrain rail link from Paddington to Heathrow opens, temporarily using buses to complete the link from Heathrow Junction to the airport. The buses are 19 DAF SB220LF with Plaxton Prestige bodies, operated by Speedlink.

High-profile but short-lived, the FastTrain bus service linked a temporary station at Heathrow Junction with the airport from January until June, when the express train service from Paddington was extended to the airport. *SJB*

• Magpie Travel introduces Green Line service 290 from High Wycombe to London, replacing a service withdrawn by The Shires. Magpie uses Mercedes-Benz minicoaches.

• Thamesdown Transport sells part of its Kingston Coaches business, with eight vehicles, to Wilts & Dorset. The remainder of the operation, with seven coaches, is absorbed by Thamesdown.

• Ensign Bus sells its 100-vehicle London Pride tourist business to a consortium led by former employees of the Original London Sightseeing Tour which was taken over by Arriva from London Coaches in December 1997.

• The Kinchbus operation in Loughborough, with 57 buses, is bought by Wellglade, owners of Trent and Barton.

• New operator Western Greyhound starts up in Newquay. It is run by a former Western National director.

• Nottingham City Transport takes over Pathfinder of Newark (28 minibuses). It is absorbed into the main fleet in November.

• Andrews of Sheffield takes over the operations of sister company Yorkshire Terrier, although the Yorkshire Terrier livery and fleetname are to remain. Both companies are part of the Yorkshire Traction group.

February

• MK Metro's Premier Buses operation (23 vehicles), serving the Huntingdon area, is bought by Blazefield from Julian Peddle. Peddle had set the operation up in May 1997, taking over from Stagecoach which had been instructed by the OFT to sell that part of its United Counties business. The acquired fleet is made up primarily of former United Counties buses, many still in Stagecoach colours.

• The first Cannon Softline chassis is delivered to Robin Hood to have an RH2000 body fitted. The Softline uses a front-mounted Cummins B-series engine. The coach is scheduled for completion in April but does not appear until October. At the same time the first mid-engined Islander chassis – a latter-day Leyland Swift – is delivered to Leicester Carriage builders.

• Kinsman of Bodmin goes into receivership. The company had been running 16 elderly coaches.

• The first Noge-bodied coach for the UK, on an MAN underframe, is delivered to David Palmer Coaches of Normanton.

• Hookways Pleasureways of Okehampton buy Jennings Coaches of Bude, taking over 11 vehicles.

• MTL gives up coach operation, selling its remaining 12 vehicles to Hardings of Birkenhead. The operation had run under the Sightseers brand. MTL had in August 1997 given up coaching in London.

• The first Midland Metro tram is shown to the press. The system is to start in the autumn – but the start date is postponed twice and the service fails to commence in 1998.

• Stevensons of Uttoxeter take over the services operated by Handybus of Chesterton. Handybus ran 12 minibuses which are sold by Stevensons without being used.

March

• CPT unveils CoachMarque quality standard. Initial operators signing up to CoachMarque are Armchair (London), Brighton & Hove, David Palmer Coaches (Normanton), Scan Coaches, Shearings, Tellings Golden Miller, Truronian and Wallace Arnold.

• Plans for a £50million guided busway in Edinburgh, CERT, are given the go-ahead. A number of groups are reported to be interested in bidding for the project.

• The last old-style DAF SB220 with Ikarus body enters service with K-Line of Huddersfield. A new low-floor DAF/Ikarus is reported to be under development.

• The last Alexander PS-type is built – on a Volvo B10M for Stagecoach. Alexander had built 1,657 PS- and P-types over a 14-year production life.

• Alexander unveil first ALX300 body to be fitted to a DAF chassis. It is for Arriva Yorkshire.

• Caetano unveil a facelifted version of the Enigma, in response to operators' reactions to the original model shown at Coach & Bus 97. The revised Enigma has a much deeper windscreen and new mirrors. Prices for a standard 53-seater are quoted as £155,266 on a Volvo B10M, £143,500 on a Dennis Javelin GX, or £140,000 on a standard Javelin. The original prototype is sold to Reliant of Heather.

• Coachbuilder Robin Hood Vehicle Industries goes into receivership. The company was bought by Buddens Coaches in October 1997. The Buddens business is unaffected.

• Oxford's electric MetroRiders are withdrawn because of a lack of funding. They had been operating – not always very well – since 1993.

• MTL buys Village Group Tours. Village operated 53 buses, including 39 Leyland Titans, and was one of the biggest independents serving Liverpool.

• The Irizar Century body is given a minor facelift with a restyled front panel.

• Ten vehicles are destroyed by a fire at the depot of Cedrics Coaches of Colchester.

April

• The first production Optare Solos enter service, with Wilts & Dorset.

• Thames Travel starts services in the Wallingford area running new Mercedes-Benz Varios.

• Yeates Bus & Coach, the Loughborough-based dealer, is renamed Volvo Coach Sales. The company has been owned by Volvo since 1990.

• MTL North is adopted as the fleet name for Merseyside Transport's operations.

• Supreme Coaches of Coventry closes following the death of its owner in 1997. At the end the old-established company had just four coaches.

• Neoplan announces that its Transliner body will be available in the UK on a MAN 18.350 underframe, at a cost of £178,000. It joins the £170,000 Dennis Javelin/Transliner combination, available in the UK since 1995.

• Blackpool Transport's Seagull Coaches operation adopts a new yellow and blue livery.

• Tellings Golden Miller buys a share of Burtons Coaches of Haverhill.

• Coach of the Year at the 1998 Brighton Coach Rally is a three-axle EOS 230 integral owned by Hallmark.

May

• Frazer-Nash, designers of electric vehicles, buy the factory which makes the Robin Hood RH2000. It relaunches the body as the Eastleigh 100.

• Selwyns Travel of Runcorn buys the Star Line coach operation from Arriva. The Star Line name will be retained. Eight coaches are involved.

• Owen of Salsburgh starts operating as Scottish Highway Express between Glasgow and Edinburgh in competition with Scottish Citylink. Owen had previously been a supplier of coaches for Citylink services.

• The first Mercedes-Benz O404 Vita coach, with bodywork by Spanish builder Hispano, is delivered to Westbus of Hounslow.

• Filers of Ilfracombe cease operating buses but continue running coaches. Ten buses are to be sold, including the unique 1992 Alexander-bodied Iveco TurboCity double-decker. The TurboCity is advertised by Filers in *Bus and Coach Buyer* at £45,000 – a figure reduced to £39,950 when it is still unsold at the end of the year.

• Iveco and Renault announce that their bus and coach businesses are to be merged from January 1999. The merger includes Renault's Heuliez subsidiary and Karosa, in the Czech Republic, in which Renault has a majority stake.

• Classic Coaches of Annfield Plain takes over the 14-vehicle Go-Highstyle coach operation run by the Go-Ahead Group. In return it cuts back on bus competition with Go-Ahead.

• FirstGroup takes over Mainline – it already had a 20 per cent shareholding.

• Plaxton announces the Mini Pointer Dart, an 8.5m midibus based on a new short variant of the Dennis Dart SLF chassis.

June

• Reading Transport buys the Reading Mainline business, running 44 Routemasters in the town.

• Geldard Coaches of Leeds gives up its Bigfoot bus services, launched in 1995 and operated by Leyland Nationals.

37

- Parry People Mover flywheel-powered tram starts running in Bristol Docks on a 1.4km track. It is operated by Bristol Electric Railbus.

- Appleby buys North Bank Travel of Hull (18 vehicles, of which 13 are Leyland Nationals).

- Classic Coaches takes over the operation of Derwent Coaches of Swalwell, with six vehicles.

July

- Plans for a £50million guided busway are approved by Northampton Council. A 40 kilometre system is planned, with the first stage to be operational by 2000. The promoters, Rapid Transit International, say that they will use gas-powered vehicles.

- Ayats re-enters the coach market. It plans to sell 36 Bravo integrals in 1999.

- Government publishes it transport policy document, *A New Deal for Transport*.

Merseypride ceased operating in August. Seen in Liverpool shortly before the end is a former Ribble Leyland Titan PD3 with Metro-Cammell body. *SJB*

- Government announces that from 1 January 1999 the maximum permissible weight for two-axle buses and coaches will be increased from 17 to 18 tonnes.

- FirstGroup buys Capital Citybus, the biggest London independent, and the associated Walthamstow Citybus which also traded under the Capital fleet name.

- The seven vehicle fleet of Miles Coaches of Shrivenham is taken over by Berrys Transport, a haulage company based in Ashton Keynes.

- The operations of OK Motor Services are absorbed by other parts of the Go-Ahead group with the phasing-out of the OK name. The bulk of the OK fleet passes to Northern General which takes 56 vehicles. At the same time the Tyneside Omnibus Co operation with 58 buses is taken over by Tynemouth & District. Tyneside's Go-VFM name is abandoned and replaced by Tynemouth's Go-Coastline. Northern General also absorbs the 16-strong Northern National fleet.

August

- Metroline buys Scottish Citylink from National Express in a deal worth £10.3million. Citylink carried 2.2 million people in 1997. FirstGroup and Stagecoach were also reported to have bid for the Scottish express coach operator.

- Ouse Valley Coaches of Bedford (12 vehicles) ceases operations. It had been established almost 50 years.

- HMB of Newcastle ceases trading. It ran 38 buses – mainly Mercedes and Metroriders – and had started in April 1997.

- Weybus of Weymouth calls in the receivers after having its operating licence revoked. The company ran some 20 minibuses in competition with Southern National.

- Wright announce a new low-floor minibus body suitable for Mercedes-Benz and Iveco running units. An artist's impression is issued, but no technical details are released, nor is a production date announced.

- Metroline buys MTL London Northern.

- Rapson Coaches buys Highland Country Buses back from National Express. Rapson already owns Highland Scottish Omnibuses, of which Highland Country was a part until October 1995. It had been sold by Rapson to National Express in January 1996.

- The coaching operations of Metrobus of Orpington are bought-out by a new company, Southlands Travel. Metrobus had operated 20 coaches.

- Mayflower takes a 40 per cent stake in Metrotrans, the US school bus converter, and importer of Irizar coaches.

- Merseypride (26 buses) closes – with less than 24 hours notice. The company's owner quickly restarts with a new operation, Liverpool Motor Services.

- Ensignbus takes over the bus operations of Eastonways of Ramsgate with 28 vehicles. The Kings Ferry takes over part of the Eastonways coach business and renames it Travel Rite.

September

• National Express buys the Crabtree-Harmon Corporation, which operates 1,200 school buses in the US, mainly in Missouri.

• Arriva Bus & Coach announces that it will be selling the 45-seat Smit Stratos body on 10.6m DAF SB2750 rear-engined chassis. Smit, like DAF, is part of the VDL Group. Small numbers of Smit bodies were imported to the UK in 1982-83.

• Wiffens Coaches of Finchingfield, Essex, ceases operations when its proprietor retires. Flagfinders of Braintree takes over the six vehicles operated by Wiffens.

• Leasing and rental specialist Cheshire Bus & Coach changes its name to Mistral.

• Volvo buys Mexican bus builder MASA, which produces around 2,000 vehicles annually. Henlys is expected to take a 35 per cent interest in the company.

• Daimler-Benz buys Thomas Built Buses, America's leading school bus manufacturer with output of around 11,000 buses a year.

Border Buses of Burnley went into administrative receivership in October, but was still trading at the end of the year. This Dennis Dart with Northern Counties body was among the more modern vehicles in its fleet. *SJB*

• Welco starts operating in Sunderland with ten ex-Chester Dodge minibuses. It is in competition with Stagecoach Busways, which responds with extra buses. Press reports say that following the arrival of Welco the number of buses serving South Hylton has increased from four an hour to 29 an hour.

October

• The VDL Group acquires Berkhof Jonckheere and announces that production of Smit coach bodies will be transferred to the Berkhof Heerenveen factory. Berkhof Jonckheere claims that it will sell 1,000 full-size vehicles and 600 minibuses in 1998.

• Volvo takes a 10 per cent stake in engine manufacturers Deutz.

• Ralphs of Langley (20 coaches) goes into receivership.

• Border Buses of Burnley and the associated Viscount Central coach business go into administrative receivership. They are still running at the end of the year.

November

• The OFT brings to an end a cartel in the North West of England which it claims had stifled competition. The operators involved were MTL, North Western, CMT Buses, South Lancashire Transport, David Tanner Travel, PMT, GM Buses North, GM Buses South, Nip-On Transport and Halton Borough Transport.

• The OFT refers to the Restrictive Practices Court an alleged cartel in Hull, following a complaint by the city council. The alleged cartel relates to school transport and involves 13 operators: Stagecoach, Abbey Travel, Acklams, the associated Alpha and Grey De-Luxe companies, Appleby's, Ben Johnson Coaches, Blue Bird, Fairway Rhodes, Lords, North Bank Travel, Pauls Bus and Coach Hire, Pearsons and an un-named thirteenth company which has since cease trading.

• Snells of Newton Abbot cease trading (14 vehicles).

December

• Oban & District is taken over by West Coast Motors.

• The Government gives approval for a £76million extension of the Tyne & Wear Metro to Sunderland and South Hylton. Services are expected to start at the end of 2001.

• Arriva Bus & Coach import a prototype low-floor DAF SB220 with Ikarus 481 body. All previous Ikarus-bodied SB220s have had a two-step entrance.

• Cardiff Bus launches Ely Value Bus to compete with Alister's Coaches. Both operations use elderly minibuses.

• Daimler-Benz, which owns Mercedes, is merging with Chrysler. The new organisation will be known from January 1999 as DaimlerChrysler.

• Nottingham Express Transit gets the Government's go-ahead. The 15-mile light rail service to Hucknall is to be operated by a consortium which includes Nottingham City Transport, Transdev, the French transport company which owns London United, rail vehicle builders Adtranz, and Tarmac. Subject to funding - £167million – the line should be operational in 2002.

New in the South East

Eastbourne Buses added no fewer than 12 Optare Spectras to its fleet in 1998 – the biggest single double-deck order in the history of the operation. Like all Spectras, they are based on DAF DB250 chassis. *DAF*

Seamarks of Luton took delivery of three Wright-bodied Volvos in 1998. Two were B6LEs and the third, seen here, a full-size B10BLE. *Wright*

Huntingdon & District was the name given to the new Blazefield operation set up in February to take over what had originally been part of United Counties and had latterly been owned by MK Metro. Blazefield introduced eight new Wright-bodied Volvo B10BLEs to help modernise the fleet. *Wright*

Among the more unusual small coaches available to British operators is the Iveco EuroMidi, with coachwork by Spanish builder Indcar. Baileys of Newbury was one of the relatively small number of buyers in 1998. *Iveco*

London Coaches, with a fleet made up largely of DAFs, switched to Volvo for its 1998 new vehicle intake. It took eight B10Ms which had automatic gearboxes and air-conditioned Plaxton Premiere 350 bodies. *Plaxton*

Horseman Coaches of Reading added this unusual 10m-long Javelin to its fleet. It has a 41-seat Berkhof Axial body. The Javelin was Britain's second best-selling coach in 1998, after the Volvo B10M. *Dennis*

Who owns whom...

A QUICK GUIDE to the major groups and their key subsidiary companies, associated companies and principal trading names.

Arriva – see page 4

Blackpool Transport Services
Baby Blues
Blue Buses
Handybus
Seagull Coaches

Blazefield Holdings
Cambridge Coach Services
Harrogate & District Travel
Huntingdon & District
Keighley & District Travel
    Northern Rose
London Sovereign
Premier Buses
Sovereign Bus & Coach Co
    Welwyn-Hatfield Line
Sovereign Buses (Harrow)
Yorkshire Coastliner

Border Buses
    Viscount Central

Bournemouth Transport
Christchurch Buses
Dorset Travel Services
Vintage Yellow Buses
Yellow Buses
Yellow Coaches

Cawlett group
North Devon
    Atlantic Blue
    Red Bus
    South Western
    Tiverton & District
Pearce, Darch & Willcox
    Comfy-Lux
Smiths of Portland
Southern National
Taylors Coaches
West Dorset Coaches
    Dorchester Coachways
    Dorset Transit

Durham Travel Services
York Pullman

EYMS Group
Connor & Graham
East Yorkshire Motor Services
Finglands
Hull & District
Scarborough & District Motor Services
    Primrose Valley
    Scarborough Skipper

FirstGroup – see page 28

Flights Travel Group
Central Coachways
Excelsior Coachways
Flights Coach Travel

Go-Ahead Group
Brighton & Hove Bus and Coach Co
City of Oxford Motor Services
    The Oxford Bus Company
    The Wycombe Bus Company
Go North East
    Go Gateshead
    Go Xpress
    Low Fell Coaches
    Northern General Transport Co
        Go Northern
    Sunderland & District Omnibus Co
        Go Wear Buses
    Tynemouth & District Omnibus Co
        Go Coastline
London Central Bus Co
    Camberwell Clipper
London General Transport Services
    Red Arrow
    Streetline
Thameslink (65%)
Victory Railways (65%)
    Thames Trains

London United Busways
Airbus
Stanwell Buses
    Westlink

Lynton Travel Group
Airport Coaches
Biss Brothers Travel

Metroline Holdings
Brents Travel
Metroline London Northern
Metroline Travel
Scottish Citylink
Skye-ways (25%)
West Coast Motors (25%)
    Oban & District

Moseley Group
Bowens
Yorks

MTL Trust Holdings
Lancashire Travel
Liverbus
Merseybus
Merseyrider
Merseyside Transport
MTL Heysham
MTL North
Southport & District
Wirral Peninsula
Merseyrail Electrics
Regional Railways North East

National Express Group
Crabtree-Harmon (USA)
Eurolines
Flightlink
National Express
    Rapide
National Expressliners
Speedlink Airport Services
    Flightline
    Jetlink
Taybus Holdings
    Tayside Public Transport Co
    Tayside Greyhound
    Travel Dundee
    Wishart (Friockheim)
West Midlands Travel Group
    Merry Hill Minibuses
    Smiths Coaches (Shennington)
    Travel London
    Travel Your Bus
    Travel West Midlands
    West Midlands Travel
Central Trains
Gatwick Express
London & Continental Railways (17%)
Midland Mainline
ScotRail
Silverlink

Northern Ireland Transport Holding Company/Translink
Citybus
Flexibus
Ulsterbus
    BusyBus
    Goldliner
NI Railways

Nottingham City Transport
Pathfinder
South Notts

Parks of Hamilton
Trathens Travel Services

Rapson group
Highland Bus & Coach
Highland Country Buses
Rapson's Coaches

Reading Transport
Goldline Travel
Greater Reading Omnibus Co
    Reading Mainline
London Line
Newbury Buses
Reading Buses

Rossendale Transport
Ellen Smith Coaches

Southern Vectis
Musterphantom
    Solent Blue Line
Southern Vectis Omnibus Co

Stagecoach – see page 14

Thamesdown Transport
Dartline
Green Bus

Traction Group
Andrews-Sheffield Omnibus
    Yorkshire Terrier
Barnsley & District Traction Co
Lincolnshire Road Car Co
Meffan (Kirriemuir)
Strathtay Scottish
Yorkshire Traction Co
    Coachlink
    Fastlink
    Townlink

Warrington Borough Transport
Coach Lines
Midi Lines

Wellglade
Barton Buses
Kinchbus
Rainbow
Trent Buses

Wilts & Dorset
Hants & Dorset Motor Services
    Damory Coaches
Levers Coaches
Tourist Coaches
Wilts & Dorset Bus Co

Henlys plc
Kirkby Coach & Bus
Northern Counties
Plaxton Coach & Bus
Prevost (Canada) (49%)
    Nova Bus
Roadlease
    National Expressliners

Optare
Autobus Classique

VDL Group
DAF Bus
Berkhof
Jonckheere
Smit

Volvo Bus
Drogmoller
Prevost (Canada) (51%)
    Nova Bus
    MASA (Mexico)
Steyr
Volvo Coach Sales

* minority shareholding

Calling time for Timeline

WHEN LOCAL BUS services were deregulated in 1986, Wigan-based coach operator Shearings decided to diversify into bus operation. Initially it used second-hand buses – notably Leyland Nationals – but soon started buying new in the shape of Leyland Tigers with Cummins engines and Alexander (Belfast) N-type bodies, the only ones for an English operator. The Tigers were superseded by Volvo B10Ms, and the Belfast-built N-type was replaced by the more attractive Q-type. Once again, these were rarities on the British mainland with only Shearings and Trent in England and Lowland in Scotland as operators of the Q-type.

Shearings bus operations were based in Greater Manchester and in Shropshire, but in 1991 the company decided to concentrate on its core coach touring business. In January 1992 its bus operations in the north-west and the 66 vehicles operating them were bought by a part of the company's management and thus was born Timeline Travel, with headquarters in Leigh. The Shearings Shropshire bus business and a further 21 vehicles was acquired by Timeline in February.

Timeline retained the existing Shearings livery, an unusual and culinary-sounding combination of mustard, cream and orange, and bought more Alexander-bodied Volvos – B6s and low-floor B10Ls,

as well as Alexander-bodied Mercedes minibuses. Optare Excels were added to the fleet in 1997, and Dennis Dart SLFs were on order for 1998. Timeline also moved into coaching, taking delivery of 17 Dennis Javelins with Neoplan Transliner bodies in 1995. Most were for operation on Highland Heritage tours, a contract the company retained until 1997.

During 1998 Timeline sold off its bus operations. This started in May with the sale to Arriva of its Shifnal-based Shropshire operations and part of the Greater Manchester business. Arriva Midlands North acquired 19 buses from Timeline – mostly Volvo B10Ms and Mercedes 709Ds.

Arrive North West and Arriva Manchester took over 20 vehicles. The remainder of Timeline's Manchester area bus operations were then sold to FirstGroup in October, along with 51 buses. Three Plaxton-bodied Dennis Darts which had been ordered by Timeline were delivered direct to First Manchester.

However reports of Timeline's death are premature. At the end of 1998 the company was still alive and well, albeit much reduced in size – with a fleet of 11 coaches.

Among the more unusual buses in the Timeline fleet were six Volvo B10Ls with Alexander Ultra bodies, built in Belfast. All passed to First Manchester. SJB

Volvo battling back

WHEN YOU'RE AT THE TOP there's only one way to go: down. And that's what's happening to Volvo's share of the UK bus market.

When Volvo took over Leyland in 1988 it acquired the market-leading Olympian and Lynx models. Volvo (with its Citybus) and Leyland had between them around 70 per cent of the bus market, with competition coming in the main from Dennis and Scania.

In 1998 Volvo's share of the bus market had halved to around 35 per cent as it came under strong attack from Dennis (with the Dart SLF), Scania, Mercedes-Benz and MAN. The signs are that Volvo will lose more market share before making a recovery, as Stagecoach's large fleet of MANs and sizeable orders for Dennis Tridents continue to erode the one-time market leader's position.

Volvo has backed a few losers in recent years. The B10L low-floor single-decker really found just two big customers, Travel West Midlands and Ulsterbus. The B6 midi quickly earned a poor reputation for reliability, a reputation which the improved B6LE never really managed to overcome. And then there was the low-floor double-deck prototype exhibited at Coach & Bus 97 under the Plaxton President body. It got a big thumbs down from operators. Nice body, shame about the chassis.

And then, to cap it all, Volvo announced in June that it would be ending bus building in Britain. Manufacture at Irvine, where a new bus production hall was opened as recently as 1993, is to cease in the middle of 2000. Irvine started by building Olympians – and has built an impressive 7,000 – to which were added B6LEs and right-hand-drive B10M coach chassis.

The plan is to transfer production to Sweden and to Poland.

But against that background, 1998 saw the start of what Volvo clearly hopes will be a renaissance.

It answered the criticisms of its low-floor double-deck by announcing in June that when series production commenced a transverse engine would be used, rather than the in-line engine of the show vehicle – a design change which reduces the rear overhang, one of the features criticised on the prototype.

The new model – revealed in August as the B7L – will be built at Irvine (even if only for a short time) and will use the B10BLE's independent front suspension. Modest orders were announced – six for Lothian Region Transport and two for Travel West Midlands.

The B7L is a multi-purpose pan-European chassis, but in its double-deck form will replace the Olympian. It will be powered by the 6.7-litre Volvo D7C engine rated at

Volvo: building buses in Scotland – but not for much longer. An Olympian chassis nears completion. *Volvo*

215, 250 or 290bhp. A choice of ZF or Voith automatic gearboxes will be offered.

Further B7L orders announced before the end of the year were 46 for London Central and 45 for London General, both part of the Go-Ahead group, bringing the total announced by the end of 1998 to just under 100 – well short of the 300 or so being claimed by Dennis for its UK-specification two-axle Trident.

The B7L will also be available for bodying as a single-decker and as an artic, and an unspecified number of the 40 Volvo artics ordered by FirstGroup for delivery in 1999 are expected to be based on B7L chassis.

The B6LE, launched in 1995, has been outsold by the Dennis Dart SLF – and by a handsome margin So in an effort to regain lost ground what might be seen as a Mark III version of the B6 concept, the B6BLE, was announced in November with deliveries to start in 1999. This 10.5m-long model differs from the B6LE in having independent front suspension which

allows a wider gangway, and in having a lower frame. It has electronically-controlled air suspension, and has been developed in close co-operation with Wright of Ballymena, the principal bodybuilder on the previous B6LE model. In announcing the B6BLE Volvo also announced that it had orders from Speedlink and First Mainline.

The competition which Volvo faces in the bus market is without precedent in recent years and in part reflects changes among operators as well as the company's dilatoriness in responding adequately to challenges from other makers and in particular Dennis. Dennis's Dart overshadowed the B6 almost from the start, and the new Trident could well do the same against Volvo's B7L.

FirstGroup is hedging its bets on chassis, buying Scanias as well as Volvos for its single-deck requirements. Arriva looks as though it is supporting DAF at Volvo's expense. Arriva, of course, owns the UK importer of DAF bus chassis.

And in the last round of orders Stagecoach, which previously majored on Volvo, ordered significant numbers of Dennis and MAN.

The one area where Volvo remains well ahead is in coaches. The B10M still outsells its nearest competitor – the Dennis Javelin – by a considerable margin, and despite the number of other manufacturers in the coach market Volvo has maintained its leadership over a very long period of time. However the lighter rear-engined B7R has been slow to find customers.

In the short term, Volvo's UK bus market share is going to fall rapidly. Longer-term recovery will depend on the acceptability of the B6BLE and B7L.

• For operation in Hong Kong Volvo announced in October the low-floor three-axle Super Olympian, marrying the Olympian drive-train with a low front section using the B7L's independent front suspension. KMB is to take 60 12m-long Super Olympians in 1999. An 11.3m model will also be available.

The B7R coach got off to a slow start in 1998. One of the first was for James Bevan of Cinderford. All UK B7Rs had Plaxton Prima bodies, the name used for a simplified version of the established Premiere. *Plaxton*

The Go-Ahead group bought 40 Volvo B10BLEs with Wright bodies in 1998. Brighton & Hove received 21 of them; the balance were for operation in north-east England. *SJB*

New in the North West

New for MTL North were 22 Volvo Olympians with Plaxton Palatine II bodies. This one carries the new style of fleetname adopted in 1998. *David Barrow*

The first new double-deckers for Blue Bus of Horwich were delivered in 1998. They were three Volvo Olympians with East Lancs bodies. *David Barrow*

CMT Buses of Liverpool has been modernising its fleet, and in 1998 continued the process with a batch of Volvo B10BLEs with Wright Renown bodies. These follow Dennis Darts with Wright Crusader bodies delivered in 1997. *Wright*

Operator	Qty	Chassis	Body
A1A, Birkenhead	4	Optare Excel	
	2	Dennis Dart SLF	Plaxton Pointer
A-Bus, Bristol	2	DAF DB250LF	Optare Spectra
ABC, Formby	2	Optare Solo	
Aintree Coachline	1	Dennis Arrow	East Lancs Pyoneer
Armchair, London	7	Volvo Olympian	NC Palatine II
Bennetts, Gloucester	3	Optare Excel	
Black Prince, Leeds	2	Mercedes O405	Optare Prisma
Blackburn Transport	4	Optare MetroRider	
Blue Bus, Horwich	3	Volvo Olympian	East Lancs Pyoneer
	4	Dennis Dart SLF	Plaxton Pointer
Brighton & Hove	4	Scania N113	East Lancs Cityzen
	21	Volvo B10BLE	Wright Renown
Bullock, Cheadle	2	DAF DB250LF	Optare Spectra
Bus Eireann	30	Volvo B10M	Caetano
	25	Scania L94	Irizar Century
	10	Volvo B10M	Plaxton
Cambridge Coach Services	2	Volvo Olympian	NC Palatine II
Capital Citybus	28	Dennis Arrow	East Lancs Pyoneer
	13	Dennis Dart SLF	East Lancs Spryte
Capital Logistics	9	Optare Excel	
Choice Travel, Willenhall	4	Optare Excel	
Citybus, Hong Kong	50	Dennis Trident	Duple Metsec
	60	MAN NL262 integral	
	32	MAN 24.310 dd	Berkhof (a)
Classic, Annfield Plane	2	Optare Excel	
CMT Buses	10	Volvo B10BLE	Wright Renown
Crusader Holidays, Clacton	8	Setra S250 integral	
Delaine, Bourne	1	Volvo Olympian	East Lancs Pyoneer
Dorset Transit	8	Mercedes Vario	Plaxton Beaver 2
Dublin Bus	60	Volvo Olympian	Alexander R-type
Dunn-Line, Nottingham	15	Scania	Irizar Century
Eastbourne Buses	12	DAF DB250	Optare Spectra
East Yorkshire	15	Volvo Olympian	NC Palatine I
	15	Optare Excel	
	9	Mercedes Vario	Plaxton Beaver 2
Epsom Buses	11	Dennis Dart SLF	Plaxton Pointer 2
Excelsior, Bournemouth	18	Volvo B10M	Plaxton
Express, Caernarfon	1	Dennis Dart SLF	Plaxton Pointer 2
Felix, Stanley	1	Volvo B10BLE	Alexander ALX300
Fowlers, Holbeach	1	Scania N113	East Lancs Cityzen
Go North East	23	Volvo Olympian	NC Palatine I
	19	Volvo B10BLE	Wright Renown
	18	Dennis Dart SLF	Plaxton SPD
	10	Optare Excel	
	8	Optare Solo	
Green Triangle, Lostock	1	Dennis Dart SLF	Plaxton Pointer 2
Guide Friday, Paris	6	Volvo B10M lhd	E Lancs Pyoneer
Hallmark Cars	9	EOS integral	
Halton Transport	7	Dennis Dart SLF	Marshall Capital
Harris Bus	12	Volvo Olympian	East Lancs Pyoneer
	2	DAF DB250	NC Palatine II
	6	Optare Excel	
Harrogate & District	4	Volvo B10B	Wright Endurance
Harte, Greenock	1	Dennis Dart SLF	Plaxton Pointer 2
Henderson, Hamilton	1	Mercedes O405	Optare Prisma
	3	Mercedes Vario	Alexander ALX100
Huntingdon & District	8	Volvo B10BLE	Wright Renown
Hutchison, Overtown	3	Optare Excel	
Ipswich Buses	4	Optare Excel	
Jaronda Travel	2	Dennis Dart SLF	UVG UrbanStar
K-Line	1	DAF SB220	Ikarus
KMB	30	Volvo Olympian	Alexander
Keighley & District	8	Volvo B10BLE	Wright Renown
Kent Coach Tours	1	Dennis Dart SLF	Plaxton Pointer 2
Leon, Finningley	2	Optare MetroRider	
London Central	15	Volvo Olympian	NC Palatine I
London Coaches (Kent)	8	Volvo B10M	Plaxton Premiere
London General	25	Volvo Olympian	NC Palatine II (a)
London Traveller	1	Dennis Arrow	East Lancs Pyoneer
London United	23	Volvo Olympian	Alexander R-type
	11	Dennis Dart SLF	Plaxton Pointer 2
Lothian Region Transport	1	Dennis Javelin	Berkhof Radial
Mainline	10	Volvo B10BLE	Wright Renown
	31	Dennis Dart SLF	Plaxton SPD (b)
Marshall, Leighton Buzzard	8	Iveco EuroRider	Beulas
Mayne, Manchester	5	Dennis Dart SLF	Marshall Capital
Merseypride	1	Optare Excel	
Metrobus, Orpington	13	Volvo Olympian	East Lancs Pyoneer
	8	Volvo Olympian	NC Palatine I
Metroline	16	Volvo Olympian	Alexander R
	32	Dennis Dart SLF	Plaxton Pointer 2
Midland Choice	4	Optare Excel	
MTL London	76	Dennis Dart SLF	Marshall Capital
MTL North	22	Volvo Olympian	NC Palatine II
	33	Dennis Dart SLF	Plaxton Pointer 2
New World First Bus	140	Dennis Trident	Alexander ALX500
	42	Dennis Trident	Duple Metsec/NC
	42	Dennis Dart SLF	Plaxton Pointer 2
Newcastle Airport	2	Dennis Dart SLF	SC Compass
Newport Transport	9	Scania L94UB	Wright
Nip-On, St Helens	2	Dennis Dart SLF	Marshall Capital
Nottingham City Transport	4	Volvo Olympian	East Lancs Pyoneer
	10	Optare Solo	
Oxford Bus Company	8	Volvo B10M	Plaxton Excalibur
	10	Dennis Dart SLF	Wright Crusader
Plymouth Citybus	14	Dennis Dart SLF	Plaxton Pointer 2
Preston Bus	8	Optare MetroRider	
Reading Transport	8	Optare Excel	
	7	Optare Solo	
Red Arrow, Smethwick	4	Dennis Dart SLF	Marshall Capital
Reliance, Great Gonerby	1	Dennis Dart SLF	Plaxton Pointer
Road Car	2	Volvo Olympian	East Lancs Pyoneer
	8	Dennis Dart SLF	East Lancs Spryte
Rossendale Transport	10	Dennis Dart SLF	Plaxton SPD
Sanders, Holt	2	DAF SB220	Optare Delta
Seamarks	2	Volvo B6LE	Wright Crusader
	1	Volvo B10BLE	Wright Renown
Shearings	20	Volvo B10M	Jonckheere Mistral
	19	Volvo B10M	Plaxton Excalibur
	15	Volvo B10M	Van Hool Alizee
Solent Blue Line	4	Volvo Olympian	NC Palatine I
Southern Vectis	8	Volvo Olympian	NC Palatine I
Sovereign Bus & Coach	7	Volvo B6LE	Wright Crusader
Speedlink	5	DAF SB3000WS	Plaxton Premiere
	3	DAF SB220	Optare Delta
Staffordshire County Council	7	Blue Bird	
Strathclyde PTE	3	Omni/Smiths electric	
Strathtay Scottish	8	Volvo Olympian	East Lancs Pyoneer
Swanbrook, Cheltenham	1	Dennis Dart SLF	UVG UrbanStar
Tellings Golden Miller	14	Dennis Dart SLF	Plaxton Pointer 2
Thamesdown Transport	14	Dennis Dart SLF	Plaxton SPD
Thorpe, London	12	Dennis Dart SLF	Plaxton Pointer 2
Tillingbourne Bus Co	3	Optare MetroRider	
Transmac, Macao	15	Mercedes Vario	Plaxton Beaver 2
Travel Dundee	1	DAF DB250LF	Optare Spectra
	10	Volvo B10BLE	Wright Renown
Travel London	21	Optare Excel	
	10	Optare Solo	
Travel West Midlands	113	Mercedes O405N	Mercedes
	45	Optare Solo	
	35	Volvo B6LE	Wright Crusader
Travel Your Bus	21	DAF DB250LF	Optare Spectra
	4	Dennis Dart SLF	Wright Crusader
Wallace Arnold	51	Volvo B10M	Plaxton
Warrington Borough	10	Optare MetroRider	
Wellglade group	45	Optare Excel	
	13	Dennis Dart SLF	Plaxton Pointer 2
	9	Mercedes Vario	Plaxton Beaver 2
Warrington Transport	5	Optare MetroRider	

Glyn Williams	3	Dennis Dart SLF	SC Compass	Yellow Buses, Bournemouth	8	Dennis Dart SLF	East Lancs Spryte
Wilts & Dorset	6	DAF DB250LF	Optare Spectra	Yorkshire Terrier	4	Dennis Dart SLF	East Lancs Spryte
	2	DAF SB3000WS	Plaxton Premiere	Yorkshire Traction	8	Volvo B6LE	East Lancs Spryte
	85	Optare Solo (d)			8	Mercedes Vario	Plaxton Beaver 2
Wolverhampton Council	2	Dennis Dart SLF	East Lancs Spryte				

Forward orders

Orders announced in 1998 for delivery in 1999.

BC Transit	9	Dennis Dart SLF	Plaxton Pointer 2
Brighton & Hove	20	Dennis Trident	East Lancs
Bullock, Cheadle	4	Volvo Olympian	NC Palatine II
Bus Eireann	33	Mercedes O404	Hispano Vita
Capital Logistics	10	DAF DB250LF	Plaxton President
	6	DAF DB250LF	Optare Spectra
	2	Neoplan Starliner	
Cardiff Bus	20	Dennis Dart SLF	Plaxton SPD
Delaine, Bourne	1	Volvo Olympian	East Lancs Pyoneer
First Group	40	Volvo artic	Wright Fusion
First CentreWest	31	Dennis Trident	Plaxton President
London Central	46	Volvo B7L	Alexander ALX400
	17	DAF SB220LF	East Lancs
London General	45	Volvo B7L	Alexander ALX400
Lothian Region Transport	1	Volvo B7L	Plaxton President
	5	Volvo B7L	TBA
	5	Dennis Trident	Plaxton President
	5	Dennis Trident	Alexander ALX400
Metroline	16	Dennis Trident	Alexander ALX400
	75	Dennis Trident	Plaxton President (c)
MTL North	4	Dennis Dart SLF	Plaxton SPD
Nottingham City Transport	12	Dennis Trident	East Lancs Lolyne
	27	Optare Solo	
Oxford Bus Company	20	Dennis Trident	Alexander ALX400
Redwing, London	14	Iveco EuroRider	Beulas Stergo E

Translink	85	Volvo B10BLE	Wright Renown
(Ulsterbus/Citybus)	30	Volvo B10M	Plaxton Excalibur
	6	Mercedes O405N	
	4	Mercedes O405GN artic	
Travel West Midlands	11	Mercedes O405GN artic	
	2	Volvo B7L	Plaxton President
Wallace Arnold	51	Volvo B10M	Plaxton
Yellow Buses, Bournemouth	9	Dennis Trident	East Lancs Lolyne

(a) delivered 1998-99
(b) includes 11 ordered by Northern Bus
(c) ordered by MTL London
(d) for delivery 1998 to 2000

Arriva was the biggest buyer of the Plaxton Prestige in 1998. Most were for operation in the north-east of England, but three were allocated to London. The Prestige is built on low-floor DAF SB220 chassis. *Plaxton*